RICHARD O. SMITH and KORKY PAUL

OXFORD

 TO

1000 YEARS OF HISTORY
IN 26 LETTERS

Signal

To Mary Ziyun Fang – thank you
for the Winnie Magic Moments in China
K.P.

First published in 2020 by
Signal Books Limited
36 Minster Road
Oxford OX4 1LY
www.signalbooks.co.uk

A catalogue record for this book is available from the British Library.

ISBN 978-1-909930-85-8

Typesetting and layout, pre-press production and cover design:
Baseline Arts Ltd, Oxford
All images © Korky Paul

Printed in India by Imprint Press

A for author: RICHARD O. SMITH

Richard O. Smith was born in Boston (Lincs not Mass). He began work as an obituarist for the Lincs Standard. Although he wrote hundreds of obituaries, none of his subjects ever thanked him. Best known for his books including *Oxford Examined: Town & Clown*, Richard's writing was described as 'a jam-packed jamboree of jollity' by TV's Dr Lucy Worsley. He has written for BBC comedies *The Now Show* and *The News Quiz*.

He lives in Oxford where he supports Oxford City, Oxford United Women and Boston United – which explains why he is miserable at 5pm most weekends.

His 2020 book *The Best Ladled Pans of Rice & Penne* ('An unexpected delight' – Christopher Douglas, aka Radio 4's Ed Reardon) contains 62 hilarious yet true snapshots of Oxford life.

I for illustrator: KORKY PAUL

Korky Paul was born in Zimbabwe. He studied Fine Arts at Durban Art School, KwaZulu Natal, South Africa and Film Animation at Cal Arts, California.

Korky began work in advertising before becoming an award-winning illustrator of children's books. He is best known for illustrating the multi-million selling series *Winnie and Wilbur*. Known only to himself as the 'World's Greatest Portrait Artist and Dinosaur Drawer', Korky visits schools and festivals promoting his passion for drawing and reading.

He lives in Oxford where he was once Supporter of the Year for the Summertown Stars Football Club.

Z for Zoo

The *Oxford Times* reported in July 1931 on the zoo's new arrival: 'Hanno the lion was at once so at home that he enjoyed a long sleep, from which he refused to be awakened by the incessant tapping of workmen's hammers.' This was when the zoo was expanding, with animals donated to Oxford by other zoos, including Berlin, Bristol and Dublin.

The zoo was located in Kidlington, just north of Oxford. Special buses ran from Oxford city centre with the brief destination on the front: 'ZOO'. On just one Sunday in 1931, over 2,000 people paid their sixpence entrance fee to see the animals.

Oxford once had its own zoo, known for a famous elephant named Rosie. Although Rosie only lived in Oxford for five years, an elephant never forgets!

Rosie the elephant and Hanno the lion were the star attractions at the zoo. Children would queue up to ride on the kindly elephant's back, and then visit the lions, camels, kangaroos, jackals, llamas, a family of five baboons, a grizzly bear and, rather smaller, a guinea pig.

Despite this popularity, the zoo closed down just five years later. By late summer of 1936 all the animals were moved to Dudley Castle – by lorry, not by ark. The most likely reason for closing was an escape by three dangerous animals!

Three wolves managed to break out from the zoo under cover of darkness, by sneaking through a gap in a badly kept fence. Two of the pack were soon back inside their pen after their brief walk to freedom. But one lone wolf evaded detection and remained at large for all of three days.

The residents of North Oxford spent these 72 hours on high alert, and then they heard of a sighting in Summertown. Understandably tensions grew. Residents were advised by the authorities to stay indoors and keep their gates locked – a literal attempt to keep the wolf from the door! Specialist animal trackers were sent to Summertown. The wolf – one of the most skilful of nature's hunters – had become the hunted. Yet still the lone wolf cunningly evaded capture. At night he could be heard howling to the moon.

Hungry as a wolf, he wandered into view on open ground in search of food. *Oxford Mail* photographer Johnny Johnson arrived at the scene and shot the wolf – with a gun. Which brought to a sudden end both the wolves on the run, and also the short-lived Oxford zoo.

Z Question?

Today the site of the Oxford zoo in Kidlington – generally accepted to be England's largest village – still retains some bars and fences as evidence, but they are not connected to the zoo. Who lives there now?

a charge of being caught breathing in class or something equally blameless. However, Newsham discovered that his birching rod was too soft to deliver the thrashing he had in mind.

This is the sound you might make if you were caned for getting bad marks in class. Not only was it once legal for tutors to thrash their unfortunate students in Oxford, but it was even a selling point to attract scholars. Oxford colleges would reassure demanding parents that if they chose a particular college for their offspring, then daily canings were guaranteed. Youch!

Unappealing as this sounds to us today, it definitely appealed to medieval parents, who were worried that their lazy sons wouldn't do any work if left uncaned.

But the tables (or school desks) were turned on one malicious Oxford tutor in 1301. The nasty John Newsham was about to whack a student – no doubt on

So Newsham left the classroom in search of a better birch. He climbed a tree to cut off some especially hard and springy birch branches. At this point, mid-saw, he lost his balance and dropped into the River Cherwell, in which he then drowned. Did the students mourn him, we wonder?

Y Question?

What type of tree, beginning with the letter Y, provides ingredients for vital cancer drugs? It is the oldest in Oxford's Botanic Garden, where it was planted nearly 400 years ago.

X for X-Rated Ex-Criminal

According to Oxford's coroner court inquests, an unfortunate man called Richard was the victim of a one-man crime spree on 27 May 1366.

Richard was employed as the servant of John Lally senior. One evening a shady character named Henry Louche (described in the court papers as 'a writer') broke into Lally's premises and stole the following:

'A bed worth 14 schillings, five sheets worth 10s, a cloak worth 11s and 32s in money.'

The villain's getaway was somewhat hampered by having to drag a full-sized bed through the muddy Oxford streets, though it certainly led to many witnesses at the trial being able to identify him.

There was one other item that Henry Louche stole from Richard during this particular night of thieving, and it would have slowed down his getaway even more. Court records say '…and he seized and took away Alice, the wife of the said Richard.' No doubt he received a wife sentence! (Quite a sentence, that; maybe worse than a life sentence?)

X for letter x

Dr Johnson's two-volume English dictionary of 1755 is rightly considered a literary marvel. Though usually recognised as the first ever dictionary of the English language, this isn't exactly true. There were predecessors, although most neglected to include *definitions* of their listed words – which rather defies our current definition of a dictionary.

Johnson's celebrated dictionary only contained words beginning with 25 letters – not 26. He didn't include any X words, a policy he justified with 'no words in the English Language begin with X'. Hmmm.

This may actually have been true, since the Oxford English Dictionary dates the first recorded usage of 'xylophone' to 1866 – by chance the same year as the *Daily Mail* was founded.

Not that Johnson had need of the word 'xenophobic', since he famously believed that 'patriotism is the last refuge of the scoundrel'. Even so, he refused to include any French words in his dictionary – so no *bons mots* are to be found there.

Despite his celebrated wisdom, Johnson actually left Pembroke College prematurely without a degree. Years later Oxford University gave him an honorary doctorate, and he became known as The Good Doctor.

And then the Oxford University Press decided to follow on Johnson's work with the *Oxford English Dictionary (OED)*.

Not that the institution always enjoyed the greatest of reputations – Daniel Robertson, the architect of the OUP's Walton Street home, possessed such a taste for sherry that he had to be regularly ferried around the site in a wheelbarrow. What's so unprofessional about that?

Work commenced on the OED in 1879, and James Murray was given the job of overall editor. He built a scriptorium – another new word to add to his dictionary. Murray declared that the project would take exactly ten years. But starting in strict alphabetical order, after five years they had reached the word 'ant'!

Eventually the OED was completed in 1928. Whereupon they immediately had to start revising it, as the early parts had become outdated.

The compilers included many noted Oxford dons, like J.R.R. Tolkien. One compiler called Thomas Blount became so bound up in his lexicography that his wife threw his completed manuscript, *The Glossographia*, on the fire. No doubt causing Thomas to express numerous words beyond the dictionary's reach.

So he ignored her for several more years while he compiled it again from scratch.

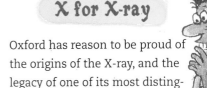

X for X-ray

Oxford has reason to be proud of the origins of the X-ray, and the legacy of one of its most distinguished women scientists.

Dorothy Hodgkin was a chemistry genius who decoded the complex atomic and molecular structure of crystals in a process known as X-ray crystallography. She was the first to prove the structure of penicillin – meaning that it could be replicated synthetically. Which led to penicillin's ability to fight nasty infections and therefore save countless lives.

Her work decoding the structure of vitamin B12, vital for treating anaemia, bagged her a Nobel Prize for Chemistry in 1964. Yet her achievement five years later, in finding the structure of insulin to treat diabetics, was arguably an even greater achievement for sufferers ever after.

Her hands were so respected they were honoured for posterity in a 1978 sculpture by Henry Moore.

Dorothy chose to keep her maiden name of Crowfoot after she was married. But then the science establishment forced her to take on her husband's name of Hodgkin, and it was under this name that she accepted the Nobel Prize. As she noted at the time, rather sadly, 'Today I lost my maiden name.' Except she chose to retain it as her middle name.

Hodgkin was not the only top scientist of her generation at Somerville College – then a college for women only. Dame Janet Vaughan, later a pioneering medical researcher, was also a Fellow of Somerville.

Dame Janet is remembered for once describing one undergraduate called Margaret Thatcher, aka the 'Iron Lady', as 'a perfectly good second-class chemist'.

X Question?

What food did Dr Johnson define as: 'Should be sliced, dressed with pepper and vinegar, and then thrown out'?

W w

W for Worcester College Whodunnit

Before bank accounts, most Oxford colleges kept their wealth in the form of precious metal. Gold and silver items were stored securely in chests within a secure room to protect them.

These treasure chests needed several keys to unlock them. Or at least that was the theory.

As an extra security measure, the butler of Worcester College always slept in a bed next to the college's treasure.

So you can imagine everyone's shock one morning in February 1769 when the college awoke to the news that several items of treasure had been stolen overnight.

For a whole week investigations produced no leads. The police didn't have a clue. Literally. So, whodunnit?

One week later, Oxford resident Lucy Smith sauntered into a silversmith's on Oxford High Street and attempted to sell some silver spoons.

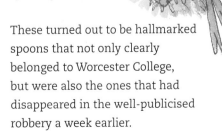

These turned out to be hallmarked spoons that not only clearly belonged to Worcester College, but were also the ones that had disappeared in the well-publicised robbery a week earlier.

Lucy Smith had been looking forward to changing her name to Lucy Bennett, as she would soon be marrying her childhood sweetheart, Mr Bennett. Unfortunately neither of them had very much money, but this irritating detail had not stopped Lucy from planning an extravagant wedding, and an exotic destination for their honeymoon.

Unfortunately, her ill-advised crime caper meant that Lucy did get to change her name: to Prisoner no. 78923. And she did get to travel to an exotic destination: she sailed to Australia, on her own – transported to a prison colony for seven years' punishment.

Lucy's gender very probably saved her life. Just five years later, in 1774, Thomas Broomfield was

sentenced to death for pilfering a silver shoe buckle from a Christ Church scholar.

Meanwhile the silversmith claimed the 10 guinea reward offered by the Worcester College bursar for information.

And Lucy was revealed to be the daughter of the Worcester College butler. So it was the butler's daughter whodunnit!

W for Wall

What evidence do we still have for Oxford's old city walls? Well, there's Longwall Street, named after the remnants of city wall, not for the long wall of Magdalen College you do actually see there. And then, where there were gates through the walls, we have Westgate, for instance. The way Oxford is laid out today – four roads from each of the compass points meeting at a central point known as Carfax – is approximately a thousand years old.

Oxford was then a wild border town on the edge of Wessex, and Viking raiding parties would frequently attack the city.

Oxford clearly needed to Viking-proof itself. So the city fathers copied a design credited to King Alfred, who had successfully defended Winchester from marauding Danes. Winchester also had a crossroads at its centre defended by a big wall around the outside. And so Oxford built a similar city wall, in the late ninth or early tenth century.

Since the wall is so important in the city's history, Oxford hosts an ancient ceremony of inspecting it. Every three years the walls are checked for disrepair by the Lord Mayor of Oxford, city councillors and members of the public in a quaint tradition that has continued for centuries.

Sadly, few remnants of wall remain, but one of the surviving stretches runs through New College. King Richard II first granted land to New College in the fourteenth century, and made it a condition that the college maintain its section of the ancient city wall. So this is the bit that now gets inspected, since it is so well preserved!

W for Wales

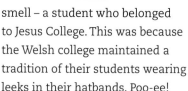

Wales has been represented in Oxford for centuries. Back in 1188, Gerald of Wales delivered some of the first known teaching at Oxford University.

Gerald was a renowned scholar appointed as King Henry II's clerk and chaplain. He was from all accounts a compelling history teacher –

by 1188 not so much history had happened, so it must have been an easier subject to teach!

Jesus College in Turl Street was known as the Welsh college. The college was founded in 1571 by Elizabeth I and her chaplain, Welshman Hugh Price. He later bequeathed his books and an annual grant to the college, though it is now disputed whether the college acknowledges Elizabeth or Price as its founder.

It was always said that you could tell – and smell – a student who belonged to Jesus College. This was because the Welsh college maintained a tradition of their students wearing leeks in their hatbands. Poo-ee!

A traditional prank amongst locals is to ring up the porter of Jesus College on Christmas Day and ask: 'Is that Jesus?' When the porter answers, simply say: 'Well, Happy Birthday to you!' They never get tired of that.

W for the woman who came back to life!

Although it's likely she was innocent, Ann Green was found guilty of murder in Oxford's criminal court in 1650. She was sentenced to be hanged.

Cut down from the gallows at Oxford prison after the terrible deed, her breathless body was transferred to Merton Street, to be dissected by anatomy students

Bodies were hard to come by for medical research then, but the University was allowed to experiment on criminal corpses.

The brain expert who was about to cut into her skull was the renowned Thomas Willis, who invented the term 'neurology'. His surgeon's saw was poised ready when he heard a sniff.

Given how difficult it was to get bodies for medical experimentation in 1650, Willis could easily have replied to his assistant's question, 'Did you hear a sniff?' with a curt 'No, pass me that pillow.'

Instead, he revived the woman, and after a few hours Ann was able to sit up, drink water and inform him of her name.

Her miraculous return to life was then seen as a sign from God that she was innocent, and therefore Ann was pardoned. She went on to marry and have children.

One of Oxford's many famous students was the poet Oscar Wilde. Legend insists that Wilde kept a pet lobster at Magdalen College, and could be seen taking his fishy friend for walks on a lead along Oxford's High Street. A good story, but probably short on truth.

However, other Wilde stories in Oxford are perhaps not so, ahem, wild with the truth. Like the story of Wilde's blue china collection prompting a run-in with the college rugby club.

He dared to declare its virtues as finer than almost anything else in life – especially sport.

Determined to smash his china collection, the college's rugby team arrived on Wilde's staircase intent on giving the man of letters a dunking in the nearby River Cherwell.

One by one they toppled back down the stairs as Wilde, with his sturdy tall frame and consequent strength, sent them fleeing.

His blue glass collection survived, as did his reputation for elegant tableware.

Wilde came up to Oxford in 1874 and stayed in the city for four years studying Classics.

He was supposedly indulging in a leisurely extended breakfast at The Mitre in the High Street when he read in *The Times* that he had obtained a double First.

W Question?

Where Oxford students live is controlled by a strict University rule. According to examination regulations, undergraduates must live within how many miles of Carfax Tower?

V for Violence

that there were tribes of Welsh, Irish and Scots. English students would divide themselves between Northerners (anyone from north of the River Nene) and Southerners. Then they would go out and fight one another in tribal wars. Very violently. That's basically what they seemed to do all day. Hadn't these students got an essay crisis to occupy them instead?

Violence between Town and Gown has been commonplace throughout much of Oxford's history. Less well reported is violence between students, which has often been as frequent and as bloody.

In medieval Oxford, students would group themselves by geographical origin. This meant

Two students from Broadgate Hall (where Pembroke College now stands) ambushed and attacked two students from a rival college in 1446 with fatal results.

In 1459, student John Smart of Gloucester College (now Worcester College) took a break from studying to whack Oriel student John Alden repeatedly over the head with a large knobbly stick. Their punishment was rather quaint – they were made to give each other a kiss of peace.

Better known was the Town and Gown violence that continued for centuries. Even by Oxford standards, things got pretty violent in 1298.

During an official parade of Town dignitaries, the mayor and bailiffs were attacked at Carfax by a group of students in an organised ambush. They stole the gold mace and trampled on it. Repercussions continued for several days: 'Full three thousand clerks [students] with bows and arrows, swords' attacked random townspeople. Many died. Yet the University Chancellor refused to punish any of the student culprits.

Another student was apprehended after an evening out clubbing – in this case, clubbing an unfortunate Oxford homeowner over the head after he'd disturbed the undergraduate in the act of thieving his candlesticks. The scheming scholar was training to be a vicar!

You can see why the Town seethed in resentment towards Gown. Local townspeople would deliberately create teetering piles of rotting waste outside colleges, obstruct their gates and charge inflated prices for supplying food.

Not even the church was above a spot of violence. In 1452, Robert Wrixham forced his way into the house of an Oxford fishmonger. Once inside he filled his swag bag with loot. When the homeowner came downstairs to investigate the noises below, Wrixham bashed him with a club. Robert Wrixham's day job – housebreaker being a strictly moonlighting profession – was that of an ordained chaplain.

Sadly violence wasn't only inflicted on the human population of Oxford. Even as late as 1826 there was an official Oxford University bull-baiting society!

V for Venison

In what other town or city can you find a massive deer park located 100 metres from the High Street? Only in Oxford. Yet Magdalen College, which owns this deer park, was so concerned that its animals were going to be eaten by hungry soldiers and townspeople during the Civil War that it had its deer officially reclassified as a vegetable.

Sometimes you can see venison for sale in Oxford's Covered Market today. Why not point to it and say: 'Expensive? That's dead deer, that is!'

V for Votes

Oxford University was a chauvinistic place for a very long time. Even as late as the nineteenth century, a prominent psychologist suggested that the amount of study necessary for an Oxbridge degree would cause permanent damage to a woman's brain!

St John's College didn't approve of its Fellows having wives – too much like fraternising with the enemy. Once members of college had voted to elect a new Fellow, they also reputedly sat to consider the suitability of the Fellow's choice of wife. This practice apparently continued until the 1960s!

Historically, Oxford University's colleges were for male students only. Finally, in 1974, five colleges voted to admit female undergraduates: Brasenose, Jesus College, Wadham, Hertford and St Catherine's.

There was opposition from opponents of progress. Fellows at one college harboured concerns about accepting women based on the belief that female students would require full-length mirrors in their rooms and thereby incur the college additional expense. In 1984 Oriel became the last of the all male colleges to vote to accept female undergraduates.

But meanwhile the women's colleges had also voted to admit men: Lady Margaret Hall and St Anne's in 1979, St Hugh's in 1986, Somerville in 1994, St Hilda's in 2008. By 2018, for the first time ever, more female undergraduates than male were admitted to Oxford.

Times have changed from when useful advice was issued to early women students in the event of unwanted attention from male counterparts: 'Don't run away. This rouses the spirit of the chase. And don't faint.'

ⱴ Question?

Oxford University was certainly up and running long before the twelfth century ended. Some give a foundation date of 1167. When do you think female students arrived at Oxford? Which century would you guess?

U for University College

Oxford's oldest college, Univ – as it's commonly abbreviated – held its 1,000th anniversary dinner before its 750th anniversary dinner. And they're supposed to be clever in Oxford!

The explanation goes back a very long way to the false notion that the college was founded by King Alfred. This, it transpires, was a tax dodge. In 1384, the Master of Univ sent a parchment scroll to the King's Bench. Being Oxford, he wrote it in medieval French.It contested a lawsuit which claimed that substantial properties rented out by Univ really belonged to someone else. Rather naughtily, Univ decided to add the totally false claim that the college was founded by King Alfred. This, the Fellows gambled, would influence ruling King Richard II, who would be impressed by their ancient foundation and therefore grant Univ a favourable royal decree.

When the court was asked to rise for the judgement in 1390, it decided upon a compromise. Univ got to keep the real estate, but had to pay compensation to the claimants. However, the Alfred myth spread and future generations actually believed in this royal patronage.

By the 1720s, a UK court even ruled that Univ was founded by the ninth-century king as an undisputed fact in law. Which could never be true, as it would have meant that Univ was founded before Oxford University itself! Much later some proper investigations took place and Univ's true birth date was discovered.

Its real foundation date of 1249 still makes Univ the oldest Oxford college, which by definition also makes it the oldest college in the English-speaking world.

Univ's tutors were not always popular – or missed around the common room. When tutor Edmund Strete died in his bed in Univ during early January 1386, it wasn't until mid-February that his body was discovered. Strete's manservant John West had 'slew him and hid him in the straw of his bed' before making a hasty departure to his home city of Gloucester – with a five-week start on the pursuing authorities.

several students sealed his door with long brass screws. Tiptoeing with a ladder past a snoozing college porter, they ascended the front of the don's rooms in the High Street and screwed his windows closed too, leaving him entombed like a ancient Egyptian.

Slightly overreacting to the jest, the Master expelled the entire college until the culprits came forward and confessed to the misdemeanour. Two weeks later those responsible admitted their crime and were duly sent down from Oxford – meaning that they were the ones now permanently screwed.

U for University College Prank

One don at Univ was so unpopular with his students that they decided it was time to teach him a lesson. Hence a cunning plan was hatched.

After the dozy don had retired to bed in his college rooms one moonless night in March 1868,

U for Umbrella

Worcester College student Thomas Coryat had a strange nickname – he was known as 'the fork-bearing rascal'. That's because Thomas shocked polite society in the early seventeenth century by producing at the dinner table one evening (prepare to be very shocked)… a fork. Yes, a fork. Amazingly, English people only had spoons and knives to eat with until Thomas introduced the table fork – probably based on one he'd seen abroad.

But Thomas invented other things too. Amazingly, given the English weather, no one had thought of the idea of an umbrella until Thomas introduced it to his grey, damp homeland too.

After leaving Worcester College (or Gloucester Hall as it was called in Thomas' time) he took up a job as court jester to James I. But he soon quit – presumably because no one took him seriously in his new role.

In 1608, he embarked on a journey through many European countries en route to Italy. Progress was slow, mainly because he walked most of the way. But this enterprise became another invention attributed to Thomas: the Grand Tour. He wrote up his travels in a bestselling book called *Coryat's Crudities: Hastily Gobbled up in Five Months Travels*.

In 1612 he set out from England on a journey to India. He arrived in 1615 – having walked there too. But sadly he died there of dysentery, and was buried in a tomb that was later washed away by floods.

U Question?

How many Chancellors have there been at Oxford University since 1933?

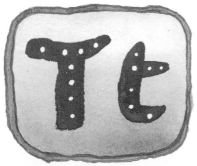

Which necessitated a complete rewrite from scratch. Hashtag annoyed.

On your marks, get set, slow!

T for T.E. Lawrence

T.E. Lawrence (the 'of Arabia' bit was added later) attended school in Oxford, then university as an undergraduate at Jesus College. He came up to Oxford again in 1911 to take up a fellowship at All Souls College. He should have got a direct train to Oxford from Paddington. Instead he changed trains at Reading station where, on a bench, he left the entire handwritten manuscript of his vast and just completed book, *The Seven Pillars of Wisdom*.

Oxford's eccentric tradition of tortoise racing culminates each year on a lawn in Corpus Christi College, where the annual Tortoise Race takes place.

Contestants rarely display any pre-race tension. None are quaking in their shells! And since tortoises can live for a very long time (they're some of the oldest land animals around), there are usually a few veterans contesting the annual race.

St Peter's College's veteran entrant is called (brace yourself) Aristurtle. It's a turtle-ly unacceptable pun.

The tortoises are released in the college grounds inside a circle constructed of enticing lettuce leaves. First to reach the Iceberg finishing line wins. Regular

T for Time Ceremony

Oxford's Time Ceremony is a tradition shrouded in mystery, and only Merton College students are allowed to attend. What happens is that at 2 a.m. on the last Sunday in October, Merton students gather under the sundial in the Fellows' Quad in subfusc (see entry for Mortarboard) to walk backwards for an hour around the quad.

runners ... ahem ... amblers in the testudinal field (no hares have entered for what must surely be an overdue rematch) are: Percy McShellface (Univ), Torty (St Anne's), Emmanuelle (Regent's Park), Sampras (Christ Church) and the 2019 victor Foxe (Corpus Christi).

Worcester's – I'm sensing ironically named – Zoom has been a victor in recent years, last reaching the lettuce line of glory in 2017 ahead of 114-year-old Emmanuelle. With an age gap of exactly 99 years between them, you have to say that youth triumphed over experience on that occasion.

Surely it's time to challenge Cambridge, and add tortoise racing to the list of varsity sports?

This is said to save us all and keep the earth spinning. Yes, it's admittedly a big claim. Nevertheless, the students maintain that their annual event rescues the universe by 'stabilising the time–space continuum' (don't worry, I don't know what that means either), while also giving them the excuse to drink lots of port.

The strange ceremony marks the hour when the clocks go back at the end of British Summer Time. They finish the walk at 2 a.m. GMT as well, which is a whole hour later, even though it's the same time, because ... oh, you've worked that bit out already. Their ritual supposedly ensures a safe transference from BST to Greenwich Mean Time, by what Jeremy Paxman once described, when introducing an episode of *University Challenge* featuring Merton College, as 'counteracting the temporal vortex'. No, me neither.

BONG! BONG! BONG!

How ancient is the tradition? Well, not very. It began in 1971, although only five people turned up. But the numbers taking part have steadily increased since then.

Initially this quirky event was secret, kept hidden from the college authorities. But later the ritual was embraced by the Junior Common Room and the college itself. Glasses have now been banned, but crucially not what goes into them, i.e. port. In any case, since students nowadays link arms during the backwards walk, holding a glass would be quite difficult.

A Mertonian was asked, 'Why do you walk backwards?' and replied: 'Because walking forwards at two o'clock in the morning in full academic dress would just look silly.' Obvious, really.

T Question?

Time for a time question: Which is the longest month of the year?

The muddled-up Reverend William Spooner of New College provided the English language with the word 'spoonerism'. Anyone know what the mord weans?

S for Stinky

Oxford must have got to be quite a stinky place in the past. Especially given the University's attitude towards hygiene. When it was proposed to the Warden of New College in the early twentieth century that baths should really be installed for the students – after 550 years of operating as a residential college – he replied: 'Why would students require access to a bath when terms only last for eight weeks?' As I said: very stinky.

A spoonerism is when you swap the initial letters of two words. Instead of telling a student that he had 'wasted two whole terms', Spooner apparently told him he had 'tasted two whole worms'.

Before a packed dining hall one evening, he is reported to have tapped on a decanter to obtain silence before announcing purposefully: 'Let us propose a toast to our queer Dean.' Awkward.

STINK

Other famous spoonerisms include belly jeans, fighting a liar (as opposed to lighting a fire), and imploring a chapel congregation to 'pray to the Lord, our shoving leopard'. He is once said to have addressed parliament's 'beery wenches'.

Serving as head of New College for over twenty years – part of the sixty years he spent at the college – he once scolded an underperforming student with the phrase: 'You have hissed all my mystery lectures'.

Inevitably some spoonerisms are falsely attributed to the Reverend Spooner himself, and many others seem improbable, to say the least. Or lay the seast, as Spooner undoubtedly didn't say.

Some of his contemporaries declared that he only ever uttered one unprepared spoonerism. But even during his lifetime the word 'spoonerism' entered the English language, and when he died in Oxford in 1930 his obituary barely spoke of any mifferent datters.

S for Sent-down Shelley

The famous poet Percy Bysshe Shelley – his middle name means 'someone who lives near a bush' – came up to Oxford in 1810. Not to study English (a subject that oddly wasn't introduced in Oxford until the twentieth century), but chemistry; and particularly the then fledgling science of electricity.

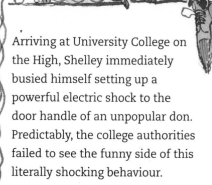

Arriving at University College on the High, Shelley immediately busied himself setting up a powerful electric shock to the door handle of an unpopular don. Predictably, the college authorities failed to see the funny side of this literally shocking behaviour.

Shelley is said to have attended only one lecture throughout his time at Oxford – which would earn him the description 'keen' from some current students. Though Shelley did remark: 'The more we study, the more we discover our ignorance' – which is a classic justification for not doing your homework.

Shelley had plenty of time for extra-curricular activities – usually involving protest and pranks. He wrote and distributed a pamphlet called 'The Necessity of Atheism', which was hardly a great strategy to win friends and favour amongst the establishment in 1811. Shelley was duly sent down.

Quirkily, the University College record book merely lists the reasons for Shelley's dismissal as failing to answer questions and supporting the Irish rebellion.

A keen prankster, Shelley was known to tiptoe out of college and come up behind women who were chatting in the High Street outside the college gate. At the time this wide part of the curved pavement was a natural meeting point for Oxford's townswomen,

who'd gather for a chat. While the women were distracted in their conversation, Shelley apparently swapped over the babies in their prams. Women, eh? You never know what's going to upset them!

Shelley died as all great romantic poets are supposed to: unfairly young. He drowned in a boating accident in Italy in 1822. At which point University College generously constructed a huge domed memorial to the poet, despite having so recently expelled him. Shelley is buried in a graveyard in Rome – appropriately next to a bush.

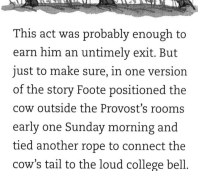

S for Samuel Foote

Arguably the most colourful reason for being expelled from Oxford University belongs to Samuel Foote.

Foote, it's fair to say, lived a rather eccentric life. He once made an unfortunate riding bet, which ended with him falling off his horse and suffering a 50 per cent reduction in the leg department. You've heard of the gambling expression, 'to lose an arm and a leg'? Well, he lost the leg, anyway.

But the reason he got his marching orders (better make that hobbling orders) from Oxford was due to an unfortunate student prank. Foote stole a cow and brought it into Worcester College to graze on the private lawn.

This act was probably enough to earn him an untimely exit. But just to make sure, in one version of the story Foote positioned the cow outside the Provost's rooms early one Sunday morning and tied another rope to connect the cow's tail to the loud college bell.

He was duly expelled – sent down, in Oxford parlance. In his defence, he hadn't got a leg to stand on!

Later, this same Foote founded the Royal Haymarket theatre in London, which is still going strong today. He provided the premises; somebody else provided the royal prefix.

S Question?

What did Samuel Foote do to the unfortunate cow to ensure that it moved around to ring the Provost's bell?

R for Riot

Stand at Carfax and, if you avoid being run over by a bus, you can spot on the south-west corner a large stone raised just a few centimetres above pavement level on what is now a bank. The chiselled message on the low stone proclaims it as the former site of the Swindlestock Tavern, where a terrible massacre started.

Two students were spending the day inside a tavern drinking heavily. It would never happen today, would it? The date was Tuesday 10 February 1355, and since that day has forever been known as the St Scholastica's Day Massacre, you can guess that this particular Tuesday afternoon didn't end well.

Two boozy students, Roger de Chesterfield and Walter Spryngeheuse, were unhappy with the quality of ale they were being served in the Swindlestock Tavern, so they complained to the publican, John de Bereford. Clearly lacking negotiation skills, their complaint mainly took the form of smashing a quart pot over John de Bereford's head.

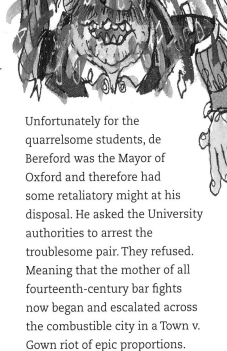

Unfortunately for the quarrelsome students, de Bereford was the Mayor of Oxford and therefore had some retaliatory might at his disposal. He asked the University authorities to arrest the troublesome pair. They refused. Meaning that the mother of all fourteenth-century bar fights now began and escalated across the combustible city in a Town v. Gown riot of epic proportions.

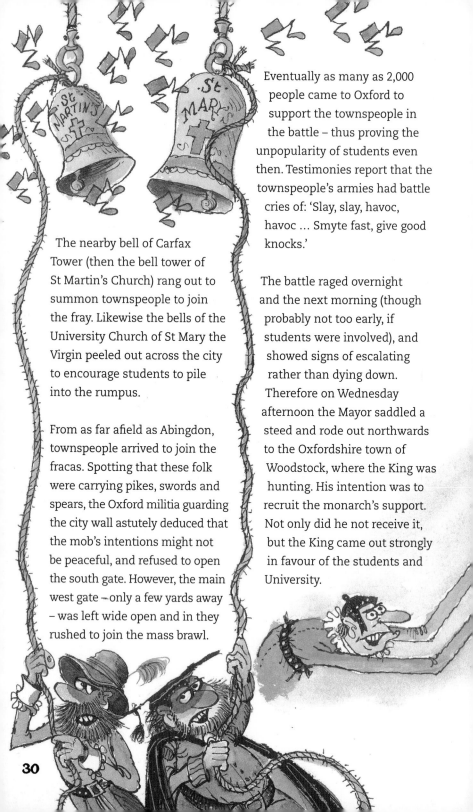

The nearby bell of Carfax Tower (then the bell tower of St Martin's Church) rang out to summon townspeople to join the fray. Likewise the bells of the University Church of St Mary the Virgin peeled out across the city to encourage students to pile into the rumpus.

From as far afield as Abingdon, townspeople arrived to join the fracas. Spotting that these folk were carrying pikes, swords and spears, the Oxford militia guarding the city wall astutely deduced that the mob's intentions might not be peaceful, and refused to open the south gate. However, the main west gate – only a few yards away – was left wide open and in they rushed to join the mass brawl.

Eventually as many as 2,000 people came to Oxford to support the townspeople in the battle – thus proving the unpopularity of students even then. Testimonies report that the townspeople's armies had battle cries of: 'Slay, slay, havoc, havoc … Smyte fast, give good knocks.'

The battle raged overnight and the next morning (though probably not too early, if students were involved), and showed signs of escalating rather than dying down. Therefore on Wednesday afternoon the Mayor saddled a steed and rode out northwards to the Oxfordshire town of Woodstock, where the King was hunting. His intention was to recruit the monarch's support. Not only did he not receive it, but the King came out strongly in favour of the students and University.

By Thursday the death toll was immense. Sixty-three students had been slain by the townspeople, and there were even reports that some of the students had been scalped.

The townspeople were never allowed to forget their guilt. Blamed by the King for the carnage, their punishment continued for centuries. Every year Oxford's Mayor, accompanied by his bailiffs and 63 townspeople to represent each student killed on that fateful day in 1355, were forced to attend a ceremony at St Mary's, the University Church, to honour the student death toll.

During the service, the Mayor had to present 63 penny coins to the Vice Chancellor of Oxford University – again representative of the slain students.

As if this wasn't enough humiliation, the Mayor and bailiffs also had to swear an annual oath to uphold the University's immense privileges over the city. Astonishingly this custom continued until 1825, when the Mayor refused to take part. But the University still insisted on their penance, and hostilities weren't formally closed until 1955, when the then Mayor was given an honorary degree by the University. The city reciprocated the gesture by electing the University Vice Chancellor as an Honorary Freeman of the city. It only took it 600 years to forgive.

Until the mid-twentieth century, Oxford locals would enthusiastically mark their calendars on 5 November with the word 'Riot!!' – a traditional day of mayhem. When women arrived as students in the late nineteenth century, the cover of *Punch* magazine celebrated the event by depicting female students getting stuck into the age-old Oxford pastime of Town v. Gown rioting.

R for Richard Burton

No, not *that* Richard Burton – although the actor did study at Oxford University. He came up to Exeter College in 1944 on a RAF scholarship. Later, Burton – we're still referring to the actor – returned to the city several times to perform at the Oxford Playhouse. During some performances his loyal dresser would stand permanently in the wings holding a tumbler of whisky in one hand and a lit cigarette in the other, enabling Burton to have a quick swig and drag between scenes. What a pro.

The other Richard Burton was a famous explorer, author, adventurer, spy, linguist, fencer, falconer and daredevil.

Burton was the first to source and translate into English the *Kama Sutra* – thereby giving more work to chiropractors than anyone else had ever done.

Arriving a whole year late as a student at Trinity College in 1841, he didn't make friends easily. Somewhat proving this point, he claimed to keep a poker permanently red hot in his fire in case any visitors required it inserted up their…

Within a few days of Burton arriving at Trinity, a fellow undergraduate insulted the newcomer's 'splendid moustache' at dinner. Clearly not dealing with criticism well, Burton challenged his fellow student to a duel.

At dawn the next morning Burton arrived promptly for his deadly rendezvous. His opponent failed to arrive – though, with hindsight, expecting a student to be up at dawn for anything was quite optimistic.

However, the college authorities were early risers and they discovered Burton's intention to duel. Inevitably rustication followed.

However, it wasn't long before Burton committed a crime far more heinous in the eyes of the University. It was forbidden for students to attend horse racing meetings. Caught arranging a stagecoach trip to see a champion steeplechaser, Burton was sent down by his college.

But those are the stories according to Burton's own written accounts. Trinity College's superbly preserved archives suggest that Burton may not have been entirely accurate in his autobiographical recollections – many of his tales are taller than a giraffe with a stepladder.

Burton's name in Trinity's surviving buttery book does not bear the scars of a sent-down scholar, i.e. the customary thick crossing out of a wretch's name to show he'd been expelled. And although Burton dismissively branded his fellow students at Oxford as mere 'sons of grocers', the book confirms that he had less money to spend than almost everyone else in college at the time. He was certainly querulous, describing his living accommodation as 'a dog hole called a room'.

Burton may well have embellished his Oxford memoirs. Yet one indisputable truth is that Burton couldn't bear to be ordinary.

R for Rebellious Ruffians

Henry III branded Oxford students 'rebellious ruffians' and ordered them to register. He thought that this would ensure greater student accountability.

The process is called Matriculation, and it still happens today each October. All students formally join the University in the first week of their first term in Oxford by attending a matriculation ceremony in the Sheldonian Theatre.

R Question?

What was Richard Burton's punishment for attempting to shoot dead a fellow student on his first morning at Oxford University?

Q for Queen Matilda

Matilda was the daughter of Henry I. After her brother, the king in waiting, died in a shipwreck, she wanted to be queen. Unfortunately, so did a lot of others – who all coveted the power of being England's monarch. Especially since the job came with a really nice bejewelled crown.

This row over who should succeed to the throne led to a raging civil war known as The Anarchy. At least if she couldn't be the undisputed queen, Matilda managed to gain herself an impressive title: Empress Matilda. Her cool empress prefix was picked up by marrying Holy Roman Emperor Henry V.

However, empress or not, she experienced some real problems with her family. When her dad died in 1135, the power vacuum for the crown attracted numerous candidates. Her cousin Stephen was grandson of William the Conqueror, and boy did he bang on about it. He thought that his royal conquering connections entitled him to claim the throne outright. Empress Matilda thought otherwise.

Matilda was not averse to a spot of power grabbing herself. She even raised an army to go for the crown in 1139, and got as far as organising her own coronation in London. But the crown wasn't placed on her head due to a hostile crowd interfering, so she never technically became a queen. Meanwhile her cousin Stephen's rival campaign to become monarch was gaining support.

Besieged in Oxford Castle for three months in late 1142, Matilda became a damsel in distress.

Escape looked unlikely and her fate seemed sealed. Plus her hair was nothing like long enough to try the traditional imprisoned-damsels-rescued-from-towers approach.

Soldiers loyal to her cousin Stephen were sworn to leave her trapped in the tower for good. Food was scarce and she shivered in the winter cold. Then, during yet another freezing December snowstorm, she had an idea. Quite a good one, as it turned out.

Legend reports that she wore an adapted white bedsheet to camouflage herself against the snowy Oxford scene. Tiptoeing across the conveniently frozen moat of Oxford Castle, the white makeshift robe disguised her as the abominable snowman. Clever. No guards saw her white figure against a white backdrop. Once outside the castle grounds, it was a short sprint to the River Thames which she followed south to Wallingford Castle.

Using diplomacy rather than swords, she negotiated a deal with Stephen whereby he could rule as king, as long as her son Henry would be allowed to succeed him. The deal was agreed and, perhaps surprisingly, implemented. Her son Henry II duly became king - after Stephen had died prematurely in suspicious circumstances. Whether there was any blood on Matilda's white bedsheet dress as a consequence, we'll never know. But she did live to be sixty-five, which was a phenomenal age for the twelfth century, particularly if you were in the backstabbing business of king-making.

Q for Queen's Lane

The first cup of coffee ever brewed in Britain was drunk in Oxford. And the first coffee shop opened in the UK was also in Oxford. Plus the longest continuously operating coffee house in the UK is still brewing today – as it has ever since 1654. Queen's Lane Coffee House on the corner of the High Street and Queen's Lane has been caffeinating passing punters daily for well over 450 years.

The first ever coffee shop to open in England was on the southern side of the High Street. It opened in 1650, and initially rejoiced in the rather non-PC name of Jacob the Jew's Coffee House, later to become The Angel.

And the first brew of coffee is attributed to student Nathaniel Canopius, who arrived at Balliol College in 1637. He brought with him from Crete some coffee cherries (yes, coffee is actually a cherry, not a bean) and roasted the seeds. When he cooked up his aromatic coffee, he was reckoned as the first ever to drink it in England. But that was to be his only first; he was expelled from Oxford before taking his exams, because of his religious views.

As a consequence, poor Quinby was locked in a cupboard at the top of the college's tower. Unfortunately, Dr London didn't think to go back to the cupboard until two years later. It was subsequently reported that Quinby was 'starved with cold and lack of food and at length he died'.

So, um, New College does have a few skeletons in its cupboard. The murderous Dr London got his come-uppance, though. He was an enthusiastic adulterer and was convicted of several crimes, ensuring that he died in prison.

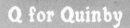

Q Question?

Rowan Atkinson studied electrical engineering at Oxford. That's right, Mr Bean went to Oxford University. But which college, beginning with the letter 'Q', did Rowan attend?

Q for Quinby

John Quinby was an outspoken Fellow at New College during the first half of the sixteenth century. His views were accused of heresy by the college Warden, Dr London.

P for Patricide

Mary Blandy was the last woman to die on the gallows in Oxford. Her demise was the media sensation of the mid-eighteenth century – mainly because the public weren't used to murderesses, especially educated, rich ones.

Mary's downfall stemmed from a forbidden love affair. Her strict father didn't approve of her fiancé, and in those days aspiring grooms had to approach the bride's father for formal permission to marry his daughter. It was a firm 'NO!' from Mr Blandy.

Hence Mary made a plan to overcome this obstacle. Unfortunately it wasn't a very good plan for any of the parties involved. She decided to murder her father, Francis Blandy. This she accomplished by spiking his food with arsenic, a poison that was detectable even in the mid-eighteenth century. If you think her plan was bad, wait until you hear her defence in court.

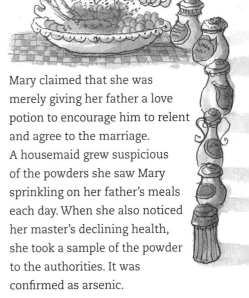

Mary claimed that she was merely giving her father a love potion to encourage him to relent and agree to the marriage. A housemaid grew suspicious of the powders she saw Mary sprinkling on her father's meals each day. When she also noticed her master's declining health, she took a sample of the powder to the authorities. It was confirmed as arsenic.

But the discovery came too late to save her father and he died in 1751. Mary was kept under house arrest. When on one occasion she was allowed out for a walk, locals chased her across a Thames bridge, intent on lynching her.

But maybe her father, who was a rich and successful lawyer, unwittingly brought his fate upon himself. He had actually advertised a dowry of 10,000 guineas to any man prepared to marry his daughter – which can't have been much of a confidence-booster for Mary. Therefore it is probable that Mary's suitor was after her cash rather than her heart – especially as the laws of the day meant that the dowry would have passed straight to the groom on her wedding day.

One thing her father did get right was his suspicions of Mary's fiancé, William Henry Cranstoun. He had entered the engagement with a small legal peccadillo: William already had a wife and child in Scotland!

In 1751, Oxford's Divinity School was packed for Mary's trial. Some thought that Mary was duped by her betrothed into believing she really was sprinkling a love potion on her father's food to make him agree to the marriage. Others considered her to be a cold, calculating killer.

All we know for sure is that she was hanged for her crime in Oxford on Easter Monday 1752 in pouring rain (obviously – it was a Bank Holiday).

Mary stepped onto the gallows and, allowed one last prayer, wisely chose a long one. Twenty minutes later, both the prayer and her life had ended.

P for Penicillin

Not many discoveries can genuinely be described as world-changing. But this one certainly can. The clinical properties of penicillin were discovered in Oxford in a famous experiment at the Dunn School in 1938.

A policeman was pruning his roses in his Oxfordshire garden. Quite a safe activity, you'd think? Er, no. He scratched himself on a rose thorn and the wound became badly infected. Lying in an Oxford

10,000 guineas

hospital bed, he was about to die when he became the world's first patient to receive the new wonder drug penicillin.

Miraculously he started to recover from an ailment with no known cure. However, supplies were so scarce that the penicillin had to be recycled from the patient's urine: an early example of a hospital funding crisis taking the p....

But there still wasn't sufficient penicillin in existence to save this first patient's life. And so the policeman's legacy was that he was the very first person to prove that humanity had a new drug capable of curing hitherto deadly infections.

The team behind penicillin decided never to patent the drug as they believed that it should be available to all.

P for Plus Signs

One Oxford man was responsible for inventing two essential mathematical symbols. And that's a matter of public Recorde. He was mathematician Richard Recorde.

Matriculating at Oxford around 1525, Welshman Recorde was elected a Fellow of All Souls in 1531, where he gave public lectures on mathematics. While there he invented the '=' symbol + introduced to England the plus sign. Which is an incredible achievement for many reasons. For starters, how did anyone set a maths question before 1531? Anything as easy as 2 + 2 = 4 was beyond comprehension until then.

Thanks to Richard Recorde, centuries of school maths tests have become possible. Which might explain why he died all alone and unappreciated in prison.

P for Plague

When people tell you nowadays 'to avoid Oxford city centre like the plague', they're usually referring to bad traffic or it being particularly crammed with tourists and students. In the past it would have been a piece of life or death advice.

During much of the fifteenth and sixteenth centuries, bubonic plague and smallpox raged in the city. Oxford's parish church registers confirm that there were twice as many deaths as births. During some years four times more funerals than christenings took place.

In 1518 Oxonians suffered from a contagious new disease known as 'English sweating sickness'. Its cause has never been established, but fortunately no cases have been reported for centuries. Oxford's sufferers were placed under house arrest and forced to display a straw sign to mark their house as 'unclean'. Sometimes houses with plague victims near schools were simply demolished.

The year 1571 saw a particularly pernicious outbreak of plague in Oxford. Often the University suffered less than the town, as affluent students returned to their countryside homes – not an option for the poor locals. Some say that Jesus College, founded that same year, managed to secure its central location because the plague had wiped out the city dwellers from that area.

In 1603 Oxford's church services were banned, games were forbidden, all public meetings outlawed and the market place was abandoned to revert to grass. Understandably frightened, many people bought so-called plague masks. These had a long beak-like design, which they filled with cloves and any other spices or home-made potions that they hoped would protect them from plague. Sadly, the masks rarely worked.

Anthony Wood was a seventeenth-century diarist whose fascinating daily observations are now held at the Bodleian. He described the piles of bodies he saw each day in Oxford being taken away for burial.

Wood is buried inside Merton College's chapel, his grave marked with a subtle 'A.W.' He had supervised the digging of his own grave a few days beforehand.

He also dug his own grave career-wise a few months earlier, when he published a libellous pamphlet accusing Oxford University's Chancellor of accepting bribes.

P for Parson's Pleasure

Oxford has had plenty of eccentric dons. Maurice Bowra was a particularly unusual one. He was at Oxford for over fifty years – first as an undergraduate, then as Warden of Wadham. Eventually he rose to become Vice Chancellor of the University. But it is his wit – and slightly warped Oxford logic – for which he is most affectionately remembered.

During the Edwardian age it was the fashion for dons to bathe nude at Parsons Pleasure in the University Parks – an enclave reserved for the practice. The spot was shielded from view by screens on all sides – except for the River Cherwell frontage. It all worked fine until one day a punt-load of demure ladies drifted slowly past the naked dons.

Panic ensued amongst the portly port drinkers, who were all in their customary bare state. Everyone hastily grabbed their towels and frantically covered their private parts. Everyone, that is, with the exception of Maurice Bowra.

Bowra calmed picked up his towel and used it to cover his face.

'What are you doing?!!' screeched the other dons, while the ladies presumably fanned themselves to avoid fainting – as ladies typically did in those days. 'Explain yourself!' demanded one don. So Maurice Bowra did explain himself, retorting: 'I don't know about you gentlemen, but in Oxford I am known by my face.' Logical.

P for Protest

Oxford University was caught in the glare of media publicity when a protest campaign known as Rhodes Must Fall broke out in 2015. Protesters demanded the removal of a statue of Cecil Rhodes from Oriel College's High Street façade. Rhodes was an unrepentant imperialist and coloniser. He was a politician, businessman and mining magnate; a diamond dealer but most definitely not a diamond geezer.

Ooops

According to the demonstrators, Rhodes was an Empire expander and baddie – believing that his race was superior and thereby entitled to own as much of the world as possible. He gave Rhodesia (now Zimbabwe) his name. He also gave Oriel a lot of money – hence the statue.

Rhodes once declared: 'Wherever you turn your eye – except in science – an Oxford man is at the top of the tree.' Which is a bit unfair on Oxford's scientists – though true about any Oxonians working as tree surgeons or apple pickers.

More positively, Rhodes funded scholarships from 1902 that have enabled over 8,000 foreign students to study at Oxford.

Several years after the protests started, Rhodes' statue still stands. But many students still think it should fall.

P Question?

Why did only three members of the team behind penicillin receive a Nobel Prize for their efforts, and not Norman Heatley whose role was also crucial? He'd helped solve the crucial conundrum of how to grow the mouldy culture – in used hospital bedpans!

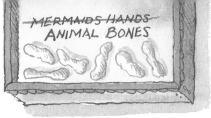

O for Oldest Museum

Oxford has the oldest museum in Europe. And you can still visit it, especially as nowadays it's free. Whereas when the Ashmolean Museum opened in 1683 in Broad Street, it charged a hefty admission price – in a barely disguised ploy to keep out the riff-raff.

But the tactic didn't work, as people were keen to see its star exhibits, including a mermaid's

hand. Later the mermaid's hand was re-labelled more accurately as some animal bones, and ceased to be such an attraction.

In those days it was called the Tradescant collection. The Tredescants were a father and son – confusingly both called John Tradescant – who must have made Mrs Tradescant absolutely furious as they collected anything and everything and insisted on storing it all in their home. At least when she scolded them, 'John! Not another piece of junk in my house! John?!' father and son could say to each other: 'I think she's talking to you.'

Elias Ashmole obtained their collection for his planned new Oxford display. Other listed exhibits that the museum was charging the public to see included: a goose which had grown in Scotland on a tree, a small piece of wood from the

cross of Jesus Christ, a kind of unicorn, a sea parrot, a human bone weighing 42 pounds and a dragon's egg. And presumably an imminent visit from Trading Standards too!

In 1894 the Ashmolean moved to Beaumont Street. It now houses all sorts of treasures, including the lantern that Guy Fawkes was holding when apprehended in the Houses of Parliament just as he was about to light his gunpowder barrels. He must have been pretty furious too – but luckily he didn't have a short fuse.

Also in the Ashmolean you can see the tear-shaped Alfred Jewel – so called because it's inscribed 'Aelfred Mec Heht Gewyrcan' ('Alfred ordered me to be made'). Alfred the Great ruled as King of Wessex from AD 871 to 899 (see W for Wall).

The Alfred Jewel was discovered by a ploughman in a muddy field in North Petherton, Somerset, in 1693, near where Alfred had been fighting the Vikings. And since that's the same King Alfred who is said to have burned the cakes, you could say he's earned a reputation in history for being a bit absent-minded. But he proved to be much better at battling Vikings than looking after jewellery or appearing on the Great British Bake-Off!

O for Other Place

The Other Place is an affectionate nickname for Cambridge University. (I assume Cambridge University is still going at the time of reading?) There are other nicknames, some unaffectionate, like … Fenland Polytechnic; The Tabs. Er, that'll do.

Of course, like rival siblings, Cambridge University is extremely similar to Oxford University – the only real difference being that Oxford is much better. Obviously.

Francis Thomas Cooper had tried selling many different products in his shop at no. 46 High Street, where a plaque now commemorates the famous Oxford Marmalade.

Originally his shop sold hats. Unsuccessfully. So he changed it into a boutique that stocked socks and stockings. But his sock stock stock didn't rise.

When hosiery failed to make his fortune or reputation, he converted it into a shop that sold tea, wine and spirits. His advertising proudly proclaimed the Crown Prince of Denmark as a customer – which was a little suspicious, given the distance involved in the prince popping to the shops in Oxford's High Street from Copenhagen.

When the tea and liquor store didn't work out either – in spite of the dubious Danish royal patronage – he instigated yet another change of business, this time re-branding the shop as a greengrocer's in 1845. This proved to be the elusive combination which would crack local retail success – so much so that when his son Frank Cooper inherited the family business in 1867, he expanded the greengrocer's shop by purchasing the premises next door.

But it was Frank's wife Sarah-Jane who really unlocked the key to global business success. The story is a bit of a pot-boiler, jam-packed with incident. Sarah-Jane had been given the sorry task of removing several crates of unsold oranges from the shop, which were now too old to sell as fresh.

She decided that the best way to save the mould-speckled fruit would be to transform it into marmalade. All 76 pounds.

Hours spent literally toiling over a hot stove culminated in vast quantities of marmalade. No matter how much you like marmalade, you're going to have to spread it quite thickly on your breakfast toast in order to use 76 lbs – nearly 35 kilos – of the preserve. Inevitably she had a lot left over. Which led to the idea of selling it in her husband's shop.

Oxford Marmalade proved so successful that within a few years

production had to be moved to a special factory in Park End Street – a building that survives to this day, with oranges carved over its door, and still known as The Jam Factory. Although Oxford Marmalade remains popular, alas it is no longer made in the city that bears its name.

O for Oliver Cromwell

After the English Civil War, victorious Oliver Cromwell came to Oxford when England was fleetingly a republic.

He marched to the Bodleian Library one day and demanded to borrow a book for his friend, a visiting ambassador. The stubborn librarian refused to lend Cromwell the book, stating that rules forbade it, even if he was the ruling Lord Protector of England. Cromwell suggested that such a response might cause the librarian's head to be removed from his body unless he rapidly agreed to lend him the book.

What the librarian did next was remarkable. The takeaway message from this anecdote is: never pick a fight with a librarian.

The librarian got a book from the shelf, placed it in an envelope, sealed it, and handed the package to Cromwell saying: 'Here's your book.' Good, Cromwell probably thought, finally some progress from the staff.

When the envelope was opened, thankfully well away from Oxford, he found that it contained a book of rules for the Bodleian Library with a paragraph underlined stating: 'No one is permitted to borrow books from the library.' What an award-winning jobsworth!

O for Oliver the Oldest

Oliver Popplewell is probably the oldest undergraduate student in Oxford University's history. He came up to Harris Manchester College to read Philosophy, Politics and Economics in 2003 aged 76.

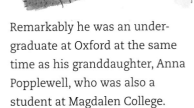

Remarkably he was an undergraduate at Oxford at the same time as his granddaughter, Anna Popplewell, who was also a student at Magdalen College.

Oliver graduated when he was 79 years old. Meaning that, like most students today, he won't have finished paying off his tuition fees until he's in his 80s!

O Question?

Which famous explorer was discovered with a tin of Oxford Marmalade amongst his frozen remains?

47

N for Norham Gardens Pyjama Incident

Eccentric don William Spooner (see S for Spooner) was having dinner in the Warden's Lodgings at New College. A storm was brewing, resulting in monsoon-like rain lashing against the windows. 'I think you should stay the night here,' the kindly Warden's wife advised her guest, 'as you'll get soaked if you go home to Norham Gardens in this horrid weather.' 'Yes, that's very sensible. I'll stay here tonight, thank you,' agreed Spooner. Then he disappeared.

After an hour the other guests were becoming increasingly worried about his whereabouts. Then they heard a timid knock on the door, barely audible above the pounding rain.

Opening the door revealed a soaked Spooner standing on the puddling doormat, rain cascading off his coatless body. 'I just popped back home to Norham Gardens to pick up my pyjamas,' he explained. Illogically.

N for North Gate

Oxford's oldest building is most likely the Saxon tower of St Michael at the North Gate, dating from around AD 1040. The North Gate itself once housed a notorious prison known as the Bocardo, from the early thirteenth century.

The prison was so unhygienic and smelly that it was probably named after a 'boccard' – an old-fashioned word for a toilet.

Poor conditions for the prisoners were alleviated by a charitable collection box held inside the nearby church.

The North Gate – and the East Gate – were both demolished in 1771 for a traffic widening scheme.

The Bocardo's most famous occupants were the Oxford martyrs: Thomas Cranmer, Hugh Latimer and Nicholas Ridley. All had the misfortune to be outspoken Protestant bishops at a time when Henry VIII's daughter Queen Mary restored the state religion as Catholicism. There was a clue in her nickname that Queen Mary was not a woman to upset – she was known as Bloody Mary. But the three Oxford bishops did upset her, and they were executed in Broad Street in 1555 and 1556.

Oxford had so many prostitutes that a special new wing, known as the Maidens' Chamber, was added to the prison just to house them.

N for New College

How new is New College? You may be surprised to know that it dates from 1379. Some of the same stonemasons who built Windsor Castle also worked on New College.

So why is it saddled with such a silly name, when it's one of the oldest colleges? Well, it's the founder's fault. When William of Wykeham opened the doors to his brand new educational establishment in fourteenth-century Oxford, he opted to call it the College of St Mary the Virgin. Nothing wrong with that name, you're probably thinking. Until you know that there was already another college in Oxford founded over fifty years earlier called … (wait for it)… the College of St Mary the Virgin. It was founded by Adam de Brome in 1326, and is now called Oriel College, named after a style of window.

This meant that among a handful of early colleges in Oxford, two had exactly the same name. That must have been a nightmare for delivery drivers. And they're supposed to be clever in Oxford.

To avoid confusion, students and townsfolk immediately rebranded it New College – and you can't say the nickname hasn't stuck, as it has lasted throughout the centuries. As did New College's poor reputation.

William founded it to educate priests, after so many had been eradicated by plague. Yet New College was the very last Oxford college to reward students just for turning up. Nothing as troublesome as studying or sitting exams was required to obtain a degree until well into the nineteenth century. Eventually they too embraced modernity and a wider academic gene pool, when the restriction of offering places exclusively to old boys of Winchester College was discontinued.

But not before its educational inadequacies had incurred the wrath of much Oxford penmanship. Diarist Anthony Wood once described New College as a stinking pile of ruinous waste, with drinking, gaming, whoring and cockfighting going on while only one Fellow remained sober. Not a great Ofsted review!

There is, however, a lovely, if rare, example of harmonious Town and Gown amalgamation at New College. By the nineteenth century it had been the fashion for colleges to display a portrait of their founder above top table in hall. Unfortunately, no portraits or sculptures of New College's founder, William of Wykeham, were taken from life. Hence New College asked the man who delivered coal to the college to sit for the portrait as Bishop Wykeham, and his image is still preserved in pride of place in the college dining hall today.

N for New Inn Hall Street

This is one of the oldest streets in the whole of Oxford, and took its name from an ancient academic hall that once stood on the site. The street provides access to the Oxford Union – the world famous debating chamber founded in 1823, where numerous famous people (including Winston Churchill, Michael Jackson, Mother Teresa, Albert Einstein, Dalai Lama and, er, Paul Gascoigne) have spoken. Former presidents of the Oxford Union include William Gladstone, Boris Johnson and former Prime Minister of Pakistan, Benazir Bhutto.

N Question?

Dressed in an academic hat and gown, which international celebrity informed the Oxford Union in his address to them: 'The responsibility of representing an entire species rests on my shoulders. When I was a tadpole, I had over four thousand brothers and sisters, so my parents couldn't afford to send me to university. Like most frogs, I could have gone into biology and majored in dissection, but I wasn't really cut out for that,' before warning current female Oxford undergrads 'not to kiss any frogs as there are already enough British princes'?

M for Murder

to practise their archery, because they accidently fired an arrow towards an unfortunate passing townswoman – some accounts say a kitchen maid, others a prostitute – and killed the poor lady.

Nowadays our definition of badly behaved students in Oxford usually relates to them being a bit noisy or intoxicated. Be grateful how much better they conduct themselves today. In older times, Oxford students would frequently murder people – both townspeople and themselves.

In the fifteenth century, Oxford students murdered each other in a dispute over a dice game. A century earlier, there was a murder instigated by students that had very famous consequences in Britain's academic history.

Two Oxford students were practising their archery in an area that we know today as Radcliffe Square. They belonged to a monastic hall of study that later became Brasenose College in 1509. The pair evidently needed

Fearing instant reprisals from the townspeople, the deadly duo fled Oxford in a hurry and went on the run. By the time they'd travelled a sufficient distance eastwards to escape revenge, they settled and decided to create their own mini (but distinctly second-rate) version of Oxford. That's right. Two Oxford rejects who were murderers both founded Cambridge University – that slothful backwater of education – in 1209.

M for Mortarboards

To look the part in Oxford, and add authenticity to the background of tourists' photos, students wear subfusc.

'Subfusc' originates from a Latin phrase meaning dusky, with *fuscus* being the Latin word for 'dark'. In Oxford, subfusc specifically refers to compulsory academic dress. This takes the form of a black gown, white shirt/blouse, black trousers or skirt, white tie for the men and black tie for the ladies. Plus the all-important mortarboard hat. Indeed the mortarboard has become a shorthand symbol and icon for academia itself.

Students must attend matriculation, formal hall, and all their Finals examinations wearing subfusc. No subfusc in Finals means no Oxford degree. Yes, that is quite serious. To comply with subfusc dress code, students MUST also wear 'dark socks or stockings' – they even have sock inspectors positioned on the exam room stairs!

However, students are not allowed to wear their mortarboard hats until they graduate. Hence, undergraduates have to spend three years (depending on the length of their degrees) literally carrying their hat around with them, before they finally get to wear it on one occasion only: their graduation ceremony. Which probably explains why there's a healthy second-hand market for mortarboard hats in Oxford.

M for Methodism

Methodism was invented in Oxford. Specifically in the quad at Lincoln College where John Wesley – who became a Fellow of Lincoln in 1726 – was observed praying in a 'methodical' way. The phrase became corrupted into 'Methodism'.

Wesley often preached at the University Church. Asked to deliver a key sermon in 1744 from St Mary's pulpit, he branded Oxford University's senior figures as spiritually lazy and apathetic nonentities. Surprisingly, he wasn't asked back to preach again – must have been something he said? He noted of the affair in his diary: 'If I have preached, I suppose, for the last time at St Mary's, then be it so. I have fully delivered my soul.'

Wesley sometimes suffered in Oxford for his religious convictions. Once, he was walking back along the narrow Turl Street pavement towards his college when his way was blocked by a notorious dandy and fellow undergraduate. 'I do not step out of the way for fools,' bellowed the rude pavement blocker. 'But Sir,' replied Wesley, 'I always do.' And Wesley immediately stepped out of the way. Zinger!

M for Martyrs' Memorial

Martyrs' Memorial is used by Oxford locals as a convenient meeting place. Yet it's an imposing monument in St Giles' that marks the horrific burning alive of three archbishops in Oxford in the 1550s (see N for North Gate).

Martyrs' Memorial is built in entirely the wrong place – it should have been erected around the corner in Broad Street, where the martyrdom actually occurred. Also, it was finished almost exactly 300 years late. Typical builders: maybe they couldn't get a skip until then?

Wot, no skip?

In fact it was built in 1841 – the first work of architect George Gilbert Scott – because of a belief among some townspeople in the 1830s that Oxford was the centre of a plot to reinstate Catholicism as the state religion. Fears were heightened by a form of high church Anglicism popular at the time known as the Oxford Movement.

Look up at the Martyrs' Memorial and you can see Thomas Cranmer featured on top holding a Bible, flanked by his fellow martyrs Ridley and Latimer. The three

bishops all went to Cambridge – though this isn't the official reason why they were burnt alive in Oxford.

The Martyrs' Memorial is also the site of a common student prank. Undergraduates like to find a gullible tourist looking at the monument, then explain that it's actually the spire of a sunken church. Furthermore, the entrance steps to the sunken church are the ones opposite, marked 'Ladies' and 'Gentlemen'.

M for Marriage

Oxford used to have some very old-fashioned attitudes. They were even considered old-fashioned during old-fashioned times!

One really old-fashioned rule was that University dons were not permitted to marry. Nor were they allowed to have houses or flats. Instead, they had to reside inside the strict confines of their colleges.

This was because Oxford University's origins were based on monasteries. Monastic halls of study meant monk-like commitment with no distractions. And clearly the authorities considered that women, and any resultant children from meeting women, and, er, anything else in the outside world was potentially distracting.

Remarkably it was not until as late as 1877 that Oxford finally allowed its Fellows to get married. From that year too they were permitted to live outside college for the first time; although a strict limit of a one-mile radius from their college was applied to cap this freedom.

M Question?

How did Australia affect Oxford University's decision to allow dons to marry?

L for Lord Nuffield

William Morris grew up in a small terraced house in Oxford. He earned money by teaching the posh ladies of North Oxford how to ride bicycles. Eventually he became Britain's richest man.

Not because he was really, really overcharging those North Oxford ladies for bike riding lessons, but because he soon became an enormously successful transport entrepreneur.

As a young man he started work in an Oxford bike repair shop.

When his request for a small pay rise was refused by the boss, he decided to set up his own workshop. In it he assembled and sold kit bikes. Adapting this same model of compiling finished vehicles from component kits, he expanded his business into building motor cars. Eventually this led to the vast Cowley car factory now owned by BMW. The Morris 'Bullnose' Oxford was his creation.

Later he became Lord Nuffield, and was such a devotee of engineering that he adopted his bedroom wardrobe into a space for keeping – no, not clothes – an engineering bench and well-stocked tool racks. His wife opted to sleep in a separate bedroom!

L for Leopold

Oxford University hasn't escaped its share of rogues. And one particularly notorious scoundrel was head of a college!

Leopold Finch was a Fellow of All Souls. He was only 24 years old when a surprising royal decree from King James II arrived in 1687 nominating him to become the head of college.

The Fellows objected to having this appointment forced upon them and managed to stall his investiture as Warden for over a decade. They had good reason to be suspicious of him, as Leopold was described as 'a man with a passion for high sash windows and low moral standards'.

Leopold Finch died in his rooms in All Souls aged 49, leaving behind his attractive wife Lucy who was aged only 18. It is unclear what he died of – though smugness may be one possible cause.

Upon his death a large hole was found in the college's money chest – money that had been raised to restore the college's chapel.

Filching Finch may have got away with stealing the chapel restoration fund in life, but not in death. The money was taken out of his probate, leaving his estate that much poorer.

Fascinatingly the college's punishment book survives and documents numerous indiscretions by Finch. After frequently 'admonishing himself from prayers', the college authorities had enough and, er, ordered him to translate a book.

Isn't it surprising that magistrates today don't use that punishment more often? 'Right, you teenage toe rags have been nicked for vandalising a bus shelter, so your punishment is to translate Homer's *Iliad* from the original Ancient Greek. Off you go.' Maybe it could work?

L for Library

Oxford is packed with lovely libraries. The Bodleian Library was described by Francis Bacon (no, not the painter) as 'an ark for all the learning in the world'. Merton College's Old Library is reckoned to be the oldest continuously used academic library in the world.

Imagine what the fine would be if you had an overdue book taken out by a relative in the thirteenth century!

L for Laundress

Wadham College was founded in 1610 by a woman called Dorothy Wadham. And yet it took the college 364 more years to admit women students. Its statutes never stressed gender equality: they stated that the only woman allowed in college, other than the wife of the Warden, should be a laundress of such age, size and

appearance as not to provide a distraction to study!

Wadham once employed a laundress who claimed to be 120 years old. That can happen if you lie about your age to get served in a pub, and live for another 100 years afterwards.

L for LMH

Although not founded until the final quarter of the nineteenth century, Lady Margaret Hall (LMH) was among the first colleges to admit women to Oxford. Not everyone was supportive.

Theologian Henry Liddon complained: 'LMH is an educational development that runs counter to the wisdom and experience of all the centuries of Christendom. It is a threat to the family, a threat to the social order, and appointing a woman as a head of college is a threat to God's own order.' And presumably a threat to whoever's going to cook his tea ...

Henry Liddon, as well as being a shoe-in for the Biggest Bigot of 1879 Award, was the vice principal of another Oxford college.

LMH was created by Elizabeth Wordsworth – the great niece of the poet William Wordsworth – with just nine students. Today it has over 650. LMH alumni include Nigella Lawson, Michael Gove, Samuel West and Malala Yousafzai. The college motto is unforgettable. It's ... er ... errrr ... oh yes: *Souvent me Souviens* (I remember often).

L Question?

What did Lord Nuffield keep pickled in a jar inside his bedroom?

K for King Charles I

Charles lived in Oxford for two years, until he lost his head over fighting parliament in the Civil War. Plus he got into a bit of bother with the Bodleian Library.

Like his sworn enemy Oliver Cromwell, Charles wanted to borrow a book, but was told by a strict librarian that not even a king could borrow an item. And the topic of the title he wanted? Tactics for fighting civil wars.

Having relocated parliament to Oxford in the 1640s, he expected it to be considerably more respectful of his wishes. But it wasn't. Or so we can conclude from Charles's own description of his Oxford parliament in 1645: 'The place of base and mutinous motions.'

Installed in his new home inside Christ Church, he moved his queen Henrietta Maria to live almost next door in Merton College. When she arrived in Oxford, toady royalist locals laid their cloaks before her and handed her a bag of gold coins.

While the University supported the royalist cause, most of the townspeople were behind the Parliamentarians. Eventually the increasingly successful Parliamentarian army had Oxford surrounded and imposed siege conditions on the city. (The reason why North Parade is south of South Parade in Oxford is because North Parade represented the Royalist North Front, while South Parade was the Roundhead Southern Front.)

But King Charles managed to escape and slip through the encircled city. He did so by donning an ingenious disguise. Shaving his head to conceal himself as a servant, he crept unchallenged out of Canterbury Gate – the back entrance to Christ Church. He fled along the side of the River Thames at night until he reached Wolvercote in North Oxford, and from there safety in Burford and finally Worcester.

Eventually the siege of Oxford was broken when the surrounding Parliamentarian army enforced a rule in 1646 that no one was allowed to leave the city unless specifically negotiating terms of surrender.

Food became so scarce in Oxford that the death penalty was enforced by Thomas Fairfax on anyone stealing it. On 24 June 1646 Oxford surrendered. Though, to the disappointment of some of the townspeople, the University's privileges over the Town were maintained in the surrender agreement.

K for Keble

Showing its relative youth, Keble College is built of brick rather than the stonework associated with many of Oxford's medieval colleges. Keble was designed in a style that architects insist on calling 'polychromatic' (that's 'multi-coloured' to everyone else). Hence Keble is rather splendidly adorned in red, white and black brickwork – although this freedom of colour offended many Victorians. Some pompous Oxonians loudly announced their intentions to plan their walking routes to avoid it.

Oscar Wilde rather harshly described Oxford as 'the most beautiful thing in England, in spite of Keble College'. More modern wags have dismissed Keble as 'looking like a lasagne'. Even harsher.

Members estimate that the place will be totally demolished in another 200 years.

Keble is certainly the only Oxford college built on bird poo. No, not the foundations, but by the building funds coming directly from guano – another name for smelly seabird droppings. Victorian businessman William Gibbs made a fortunate scraping up bird's mess in South America and selling it as fertiliser. Poo in Peru enabled him to donate sufficient funds to build Keble's decorative chapel.

Unfortunately, the decorative brickwork has been targeted by a rival college. Naughty nearby students at St John's College formed the (officially banned) Nick a Brick Society. Membership is reputedly available for a term for stealing a common red brick, a year for removing a rarer white brick, and life for nicking a black brick from the top of the building.

But Keble was to have the last laugh over its Victorian critics and stuffy medieval predecessors.

The founders hatched a plan to bring all the other Oxford colleges down to size. Ever since Christ Church was founded (orginally as Cardinal's College) in 1524, Cardinal Wolsey's college (you can still see Wolsey's original cardinal's hat displayed in the college library) had boasted the longest hall of any Oxford college. But when Keble was built in 1870, it's said the architect's brief was to ensure that it had a longer hall than all rival Oxford colleges. And so it does. If you measure Keble's hall today, you'll find it's exactly 127 feet long. Making it one foot longer than Christ Church's hall!

K for Kindle

Joining the Bodleian Library involves having to repeat out loud an oath, like making a court appearance. All new library users pledge have to pledge: 'I hereby undertake not to bring into the Library or kindle therein, any fire or flame, and I promise to obey all rules of the Library.'

Which is not very modern, is it? Not being able to read with a Kindle in the library. Oh, I may have misunderstood.

As a copyright library, the Bodleian can claim a free copy of every book published in Britain and Ireland. That means that 1,000 more books arrive every day! A new warehouse opened in Swindon in 2010 to house eight million volumes.

K Question?

Who was the shortest ever royal monarch? (a) Charles I (b) Queen Victoria (c) Queen Anne (d) Charles II?

J for Jail Fever

The defendant then issued a curse upon the entire court. They may have laughed, but within a week they were all dead.

Rowland Jenkes, described as 'a saucy foul-mouthed bookseller', was on trial in 1577 for having uttered 'scandalous words against the Queen'. He added some more saucy and scandalous words during his trial, causing the judge to hammer his gavel like a blacksmith with an over-filled orders book.

Obviously, curses are irrational nonsense. Right? But after a few days, many people who had been in court to see Jenkes despatched to the gallows for insurrection began to die.

Forty days after the trial, about 300 people had joined Jenkes in the Oxford earth, including presiding judicial dignitaries such as Sir Robert Bell, Lord Chief Baron of the Exchequer, Sir Robert D'Oyly of Merton and the Lord High Sheriff. Nearly everyone who was in the court that day, as well as the adjoining prison, was dead.

Today a plaque in the County Hall near Oxford Castle commemorates 'this spot unhappily famous in history' where the outbreak occurred. It became known as the Black Assize.

J for John the Baptist's College

Lots of Oxford and Cambridge colleges were founded by kings, queens and archbishops. St John's College in Cambridge is so posh that it has special permission from the queen to serve swan for dinner.

But you won't find that on the menu in St John's College in Oxford. This college was founded in 1555 by a trades-man: a mere tailor from

Reading. Just like his father he was a cloth merchant, named Thomas White. Mind you, he became quite a rich clothier. That's because he had one very good business idea that would have been a big hit if he'd pitched it to the Tudor Dragons' Den.

Realising that Tudor homes were very draughty places, White added fur linings inside cloaks. These flew off the rails and made him a fortune. He then instigated pioneering trade routes with Russia for his cloth and furs. Although twice his ship to Russia got trapped in ice. Luckily the crew had lots of furry cloaks on board to keep them warm.

Thomas became so rich that 1553 he was appointed Mayor of London and knighted by Queen Mary. Yet he still had one big ambition unmet. He wanted to found a college. Thomas even had a dream that he would find an ideal location in Oxford for his college near to a line of trees.

that beardy tyrant Henry VIII later took violent exception to the power and wealth of the monasteries. By the mid-sixteenth century he'd claimed it as a possession of Christ Church – the college Henry had re-founded in Oxford.

When he travelled to the city, it's rumoured that he recognised a building in St Giles' from his dream. And descendants of those trees are said to be still surviving outside the college today.

The building that Thomas thought appeared in his dream was a former monastery where Cistercian monks once studied, called St Bernard's. Although founded by the Archbishop of Canterbury in 1437,

Thomas managed to buy the building from Christ Church in 1555 and named his new college after John the Baptist, who was the patron saint of his profession: tailors.

By 1557 the first students were ready to move in. But it must have been very draughty after Henry VIII had dissolved it. Perhaps Thomas had lots of warm fur-lined cloaks to sell to the students?

J for John's Lawn

Oxford colleges uphold a tradition of having perfectly manicured lawns. One day a loud American tourist, uninhibited by politeness, arrived in the front quad of St John's College and rather rudely summoned a toiling gardener. 'Yes?' asked the gardener. 'Tell me, buddy,' began the tourist, 'what is the secret to all your swell lawns here in Ox-ford?' The gardener – whose name, according to one source, is identified as John – replied that he could tell the somewhat brash visitor the secret, but it would cost him £5.

After no doubt muttering something about Mickey Mouse money, the brazen tourist dismissively handed over a fiver. 'OK, I'll reveal the secret of the perfectly manicured Oxford lawns,' began John. 'You may want to take notes,' he added.

The American got out his pocket book and began taking dictation. 'Firstly,' said the gardener, 'you need to roll the lawn. Then roll it some more.' 'Roll it some more,' repeated the tourist as he wrote it down. 'Then you roll it some more,' continued John, 'then you roll some more, then you roll it and you roll it and you roll it and you roll it and you roll it and in exactly 450 years' time you'll get a lawn exactly like this.' Which is entirely true, though probably not that helpful.

J Question

John Betjeman was a Poet Laureate and defender of Britain's architecture. But what surprising Oxford misfortune do John Benjamin, Dr Samuel Johnson, Percy Shelley, Edward Gibbon, Edmund Halley and explorer Richard Burton all have in common?

I for Inventor

An uneducated Oxford pastry cook became the first Englishman to fly. James Sadler worked in a cake shop in Oxford's High Street – a mere scone's throw away from the parish church of St Peter's in the East where he was christened and buried. Sadler was an aeronaut, inventor and audacious pioneer. He designed, built and piloted the first ever hot air balloon flown by an Englishman.

Taking off from Merton Fields in Oxford in October 1784, Sadler flew a distance of six miles northwards until he landed at Water Eaton – which would have been really handy for getting the Park & Ride bus back to Oxford. Sadler intended to have a longer first flight, but he carelessly dropped overboard the toasting fork he needed for stoking the fire to inflate the balloon.

An undisputed man of science, Sadler was also a reckless death-defying daredevil. He regularly took off in gales, crashed into hillsides and plopped into seas. He lived his life like an eighteenth-century version of *Jackass: the Movie*. Ironically, he died peacefully at the then grand old age of 75 in 1828.

I for Imposter

Oxford clerk John Deydras was feeling like a lot of Edward II's subjects in early-fourteenth-century England: he didn't much like his king. Whereas most people were satisfied with merely grumbling about it in private, Deydras decided to do something about it. Something quite spectacular.

He declared himself as the true King of England, and branded Edward II as an imposter. If a friend had delivered a calming word in Deydras' ear, then he might have discontinued his dangerous plan – given Edward II's fearsome reputation for executing anyone who showed the slightest dissent. But that wouldn't have stopped Deydras, as he had a firm belief that he was the true king.

Deydras suggested deciding the claim via one-to-one combat. This, he reasoned, would establish who deserved to wear the English crown. Unfortunately for the pretender Deydras, Edward II had his guards imprison him as soon as he arrived.

Later Deydras confessed to making up the plot while walking across Christ Church Meadow, using a rarely used defence. He stated that his cat was really the devil in disguise, and it was his feline friend who had persuaded him to try the I'm-the-real-king scam. Deydras was swiftly executed, and Edward II even had the unfortunate cat hanged at the gallows too.

Oh, and Deydras also had an ear missing. Indeed, it was this missing ear that led him to believe he was the real King of England. Deydras was adamant that when he'd been very small – and the real king, of course – an inattentive royal nurse had allowed his ear to be bitten off by a pig. Fearing she'd be executed for negligence, she switched the infant with a nearby commoner child who was now the grown-up Edward II. Rumour soon spread that Deydras might be the rightful king, particularly as he was better looking and possessed manners, airs and graces more befitting a king than the reportedly uncouth and vulgar Edward II.

You could even say that Deydras had made a right pig's ear of his bogus claim.

In 1318, Deydras turned up at the royal residence of Beaumont Palace. (This palace was built by Henry I in 1130 just outside the North Gate; it is now comm- emorated by Beaumont Street.)

I Question?

Which two English kings were born in Oxford in Beaumont Palace?

H for Highwaymen

Shotover Hill was a royal forest from the time of the Domesday Book. A high point above Oxford, it still affords pleasing vistas of the undulating Oxfordshire countryside on the edge of the modern city – views of prancing deer, rolling hills, hurrying hares and, er, approaching stagecoaches filled with rich passengers to rob.

In the eighteenth century Shotover was the workplace of choice for many a notorious highwayman, even though the cost of being caught would be the leading role in a public hanging.

The turnpike was so steep when reaching Shotover that stagecoach passengers were expected to get out and walk while the driver dismounted and led the horses to the summit on foot. This left the stagecoach vulnerable to robbery.

John Wesley, founder of Methodism, was robbed by highwaymen in Shotover in 1737 on his way to Lincoln College, where he was a Fellow.

So many Oxford students supplemented their 'grants' by being part-time highwaymen that the Oxford execution site became known as Gownsmen's Gallows throughout the seventeenth and eighteenth centuries. That's right

– many Oxford students were hanged for being highwaymen. That's a whole load of tuition fees that won't be paid back!

H for Harry Potter's Wand

Oxford was the chosen location for lots of settings and objects in the Harry Potter movies: from the shrunken heads in the Pitt Rivers Museum (featured in *The Prisoner of Azkaban*) to the cloisters in New College where the bully Malfoy is turned into a ferret in *The Goblet of Fire*.

Christ Church was one of the favourite locations. The college's vaulted gothic staircase features in *The Philosopher's Stone* and *The Chamber of Secrets*, while the college's Great Hall is the instantly recognisable inspiration for Hogwarts' Hall.

You can also find Harry Potter's wand in Christ Church – for sale in the cathedral gift shop. One

outraged lady sent a rather fierce letter about it to a former Dean of the college. She was aggrieved that a religious place such as Christ Church (the college's chapel doubles as Oxford's cathedral) should be selling something like a wizard's wand – an object associated with black magic. She berated the Dean over several scrawled pages.

The Dean responded courteously, pointing out that although the cathedral gift shop did stock the wands, he was able to reassure the lady that they were not items of black magic. He knew this as, he informed her, 'I've tried every one of the magic wands and I'm pleased to report that none of them works.'

H for Hanged Offenders

You can still see Giles Covington today. He's been hanging around Oxford for a while – since 1791, to be exact. Poor Giles had a date with the hangman and was hanged at Oxford jail after being found guilty of murdering a travelling salesman and swiping his cash.

Historical documents detail what happened next to Covington's body. A 'Dr Pegge' took the corpse to Christ Church Anatomy School. That original dissecting room is still in regular use today – for lunch. Just don't order the offal.

In that room Covington had his insides dissected for the purposes of medical lectures. Then his skeleton was retained. Nowadays it's hanging (sorry, Giles) in Oxford Museum.

But was Covington a murderer? He certainly relieved an Oxfordshire church of its silver and raided the odd clothesline – but he always maintained he was innocent of murder. Even on the gallows he threw out a piece of paper saying he didn't commit the murder for

which he was about to die. But the hangman refused to read it out to the crowd.

Covington may have been telling the truth. A whole gang of four were accused of the murder. But one of them, an army deserter, provided a cut-throat defence. And it was his uncorroborated testimony that resulted in the other three being hanged, while the turncoat walked free with a sizable cash reward.

Covington then spent a quiet century hanging (sorry again, Giles) around the Bone Room wearing the simple label 'Englishman'. It must have been his quiet, reserved manner and determination not to cause a fuss that led staff to conclude he was an Englishman.

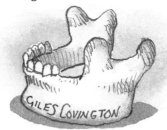

GILES COVINGTON

Then in the 1980s a museum worker spotted a name lightly scratched on the skeleton's left mandible: 'Giles Covington'. Today he lives in Oxford's Town Hall Museum collection.

H for Halley's House

Edmund Halley came up to The Queen's College in 1673, aged only 16 – not unusual for the period. However, he left Oxford without a degree in 1676.

In 1703 Halley was appointed Savillian Professor of Geometry and returned to the city. He added an observatory to the top of his house – and he was evidently quite good at DIY as his structure is still visible today in New College Lane. Yet he did not see the famous comet that bears his name, from there or anywhere else; his skill was more in predicting comets than actually observing them. This got him elected as a Fellow of the Royal Society at the age of 22.

Yet there is more to Halley than his comet. He invented the diving bell, the actuarial table and even patented a machine for keeping fish fresh. (The last one didn't

work.) But his pioneering work on gauging the saltiness of the sea dared to suggest that the earth was unimaginably older than the Bible's account.

Irish Archbishop James Usher had calculated in 1654 from Biblical dates that the earth had been created on Sunday 26 October 4004 BC. Which was unlikely, as wasn't Sunday supposed to be God's day off? Yet Usher even provided the time: 9 a.m. Hence the world was 5,658 years old. This was deemed a sufficiently impressive scholarly feat for Oliver Cromwell to allow Usher to be buried in Westminster Abbey. But Usher's calculation turned out to be the slightest, tiniest bit out – well, just by 4.5 billion years. Halley dared to challenge Usher's accepted conclusion.

Halley also aided his great science contemporary, Isaac Newton, in Cambridge. The resulting book, *Principia Mathematica*, forged Newton's reputation, but its journey into print was a fraught one. Newton may have been a scientific genius, but he couldn't resist speculating on the South Sea Bubble – even though he could see it was nothing more than a dangerous investment gamble. Newton lost almost his entire fortune in this stock market folly. Surely if there's one man who ought to know that what goes up inevitably comes down, it's Isaac Newton, right?

Halley succeeded John Flamsteed as the Astronomer Royal in 1722 – a position he held until his death. However, when Halley arrived at Greenwich to take up the prestigious post, he found an empty observatory as Flamsteed's widow had sold off all the equipment and telescopes!

Halley stepped in, helped to pay for the publication of the book and even proofread it. But Halley's contribution didn't end particularly well either. The Royal Society had offered to help fund his part of the enterprise, but it ended up paying him not in cash, but instead with several hundred unsold copies of its own over-ambitious publication on the history of fish.

Halley died in 1742, immediately after drinking just one glass of claret, contrary to the strict orders of his doctor. Another sixteen years later, the comet re-appeared – just as he had predicted. Ever since, it's been known as Halley's Comet.

H for Hall

The origins of Oxford colleges are to be found in the city's academic halls. Halls pre-dated colleges, and were composed – as the name suggests – of a hall where early Oxford scholars would eat, sleep and study. Often they were built with a fire in the middle ventilated by a central open chimney (Lincoln College, founded in 1427, is a rare survivor from the period.)

Oxford was a dangerous place in medieval times, and these halls kept scholars safe from the locals, who often perceived them as rich, privileged and aloof – and prime targets to be robbed!

The only surviving thirteenth-century hall still incorporating the word 'hall' rather than 'college' in its name is St Edmund Hall. This Hall was founded by St Edmund of Abingdon. When messengers arrived in Oxford to inform him he had been appointed an archbishop, he simply told them: 'Go away, I'm reading.' How very Oxford.

join the HLS then you allegedly have just one *raison d'être*: to paint as much of hated neighbouring Trinity College's property lime green as you can.

Once some Balliol students succeeded in repainting Trinity's boathouse that colour. Well, it's either spend your time at Oxford productively, or get a degree!

Trinity got its own back on Balliol by secretly planting some bulbs under the college lawn. When the bulbs flowered the following spring, they spelt out a distasteful message about Balliol. Isn't it wonderfully civilised that in Oxford insults are horticulturally based?!

H for Harry Lime Society

Naughty students stoking college rivalries is an Oxford tradition. Some Balliol students have taken this to extremes and founded the Harry Lime Society – named after a character created by Graham Greene, a Balliol alumnus. If you

H Question?

Henry Mainwaring was a student at Brasenose and Francis Verney attended Trinity College. What profession did both men pursue after leaving Oxford University?

G for Goldilocks

Poet Robert Southey did well to study at Balliol College, especially after he had been expelled from posh Westminster School. The reason for his expulsion? He'd written an article in the school's newsletter in which he came out against public flogging. Obviously there was no place for dangerous ultra-liberalism like that breaking out in one of Britain's top educational institutions, so Southey had to go.

Perhaps unsurprisingly, given his early experiences of educational justice, he soon became a political radical and enthusiastically launched a utopian commune amusingly known as a pantisocracy (no sniggering).

Later, Southey became famous as one of the Lake Poets. This group, best known for its members Wordsworth and Coleridge, regularly swanned and preened around the Lake District. You might be surprised that such a poet's greatest contribution to literature was actually the classic children's story *Goldilocks and the Three Bears*, first published by Southey in 1837.

G for Gargoyle and Grotesque

Look up in Oxford and it won't be long before you spot a gargoyle (or an angry stony-faced person you've just bumped into).

Gargoyles are quirky stone figures that frown down from some of Oxford's oldest gutters. In New College Lane you can spot a row of funny-faced creatures on the

southern side of New College. Here they look down on what was in medieval times a big stinky outside toilet. That's why, when the gargoyles were added much later, some are said to have pained expressions chiselled onto their faces in response to the unpleasant odours rising to meet their noses.

On the side of Exeter College in Turl Street, just to the right of the college entrance, there's a lovely gargoyle tribute. Look up here and can you spot a stone carving of a marigold? Next there's an archer to its right. Then a roundel. Followed by an eye, lion, yew and Neptune. After that there's a bell, unicorn, twins, lamb, ear and a Roman nose. Have you cracked the code yet?

The first letter of each carving spells out the name of a former Rector of Exeter College: Marilyn Butler. She was the first woman to be appointed head of a formerly all-male Oxford college.

Facing west on the Bodleian Library are several gargoyles sunning themselves. As it's a library, there's a bookish theme. Aslam the lion, Tweedledum and Tweedledee and three men in a boat (from Jerome K. Jerome's story) all keep guard over the courtyard below.

Elsewhere you can find funny characters pulling faces or picking their noses. At St Edmund Hall, a former Dean appears in stone next to his faithful Labrador. One of the chisellers of Oxford's famous

gargoyles, Michael Groser, even appears preserved in gargoyle format himself: you can see his stonework self-portrait on the tower of Teddy Hall's library.

The term gargoyle comes from a French word *gargouille*, originating in the word for throat – it's the origin of the English word 'gargle'. It's still sometimes used in France today to describe the rumbling sound your tummy makes when it's hungry. And that's understandable, since gurgling and gargling suggest the sound of swirling water being released from a building. Because to be true gargoyles, the stone creatures must be functional as well as decorative – releasing rainwater, usually via a spout.

If a carved creature doesn't assist with removing water from a building, then it's called (rather rudely) a grotesque.

Norris and Ross McWhirter were twins who did many things together. They both applied to, and were accepted by, Trinity College at the same time.

Norris officiated at the Iffley Road running track in May 1954 on the very day when Roger Bannister became the first person to run a mile inside four minutes. Norris was the official timekeeper, stop-watch operative and results announcer.

This experience forged a lifelong interest in records, and the twins founded the *Guinness Book of Records* after they were recommended for the job by their Oxford friend Chris Chataway, who had been at Magdalen when they attended Trinity. Chataway had been Bannister's pacesetter in the famous record-breaking race.

Chataway (with a name like that, we can assume he was quite talkative) had been talking to Sir Hugh Beaver. Beaver was involved with the Guinness brewery, and during a weekend's shooting in Ireland he'd missed a plover.

This sparked a fierce debate on which species was the fastest game bird. Unable to find any reference books that answered the question, Beaver assumed that there must be nightly debates in pubs and around dinner tables over similar questions. So he commissioned the McWhirter brothers to produce a definitive book of records, cautiously printing 1,000 copies and planning to give them all away for free.

It became one of the world's biggest selling books of all time. And that's a record-breaker!

G for the Great Fire of Oxford

London had a famous fire in 1666. It was so bad that the diarist Samuel Pepys was forced to bury his parmesan cheese in case it melted.

Oxford also had its own great fire, when a soldier barbecuing a stolen pig burned down a large part of the city.

Fire was a big problem in historic towns, as the buildings were made of combustible materials like timber and thatch. As the density increased in ever-expanding towns, the threat rose. A law was passed that enforced Oxford's homeowners to line their chimneys with mud – or other non-flammable material – and change their roofs to slate or stone tiles.

In 1637 an order banned all thatched roofs in Oxford. A hefty £5 fine was imposed on any thatch-dwelling householders. Similarly, chimneys had to be swept four times a year by law – or incur a fine.

Yet one Sunday afternoon in 1644 proved that even these measures were not enough. A Civil War soldier billeted in a house in Cornmarket had stolen a pig and decided to spit roast it.

This was bad news for the pig, but equally bad news for Oxford. Because the soldier's inexpert cooking attempt set his makeshift kitchen alight.

Weather conditions on 6 October 1644 were ideal for spreading the fire, and soon it was out of control. A strong wind fanned the flames, projecting the fire quickly from the North Gate along George Street. Then it destroyed most of the buildings behind Cornmarket Street all the way to New Inn Hall Street. The northerly wind sent it on to Butcher Row (now Queen Street) and Pembroke Street.

The fire claimed seven pubs and twelve bakeries amongst its toll. Over eighty houses were destroyed in St Ebbes, before the flames reached the River Thames and ravaged properties in five separate parishes. After raging for ten hours, it was finally extinguished around midnight. Such was the impact on the city that nearly twenty years later relief collections were still being made for the victims' families.

G Question?

An alderman was hauled before the University court after the Great Fire and fined for having on his thatched roof a low chimney made of what material?

F for Folly Bridge

The folly that named Folly Bridge belonged to Roger Bacon. He was a thirteenth-century Oxford genius – a writer, philosopher, inventor, astronomer and all-round clever clogs. His work on optics led to him developing efficient lenses, so he's often credited with inventing the magnifying glass.

Bacon lived in an octagonal tower house at the southern end of the Thames bridge into Oxford, and this choice of eccentric abode survives him, as locals renamed the bridge after it. Alas, Folly Bridge's folly didn't impress everyone, and the city demolished

it in 1779. But then Joseph Caudwell, an eccentric Oxford accountant, built the crenellated Caudwell's Castle on Folly Bridge island in 1849, so the name of Folly Bridge still seems totally apt.

It is said (which is a different from proven) that Bacon organised a prank to demonstrate the effortless superiority of Oxford over Cambridge. When a delegation of Cambridge students arrived in Oxford, Bacon dressed up some of Oxford's finest dons as street beggars, so that they could greet the Cambridge visitors by conversing in Greek and Latin – just to show the Other Place that in Oxford even the vagrants were first-rate intellectuals.

F for Funeral (sort of!)

But not a proper one. F is for a Funeral held after no one has died! Confused? So were many Oxford locals who witnessed them.

In Oxford they're known as mock funerals. The practice was fairly widespread at the beginning of the twentieth century – much to the irritation of the college authorities. Whenever a misbehaving student had committed an offence so serious that he was sent down from Oxford University (it was always a 'he' in those days), his friends would escort the miscreant on his final departure from college to the railway station. All that was being laid to rest was his university career.

Some of these mock cortèges trundled slowly down the High, and the processions – complete with student pallbearers – were understandably mistaken by the public for real funerals. Passers-by would often respectfully remove their hats.

This final journey to the station took the form of a funeral procession. Students would dress as undertakers, leading a procession of black-plumed horses pulling a cart draped in black cloth and carrying a real coffin. In the more macabre examples, the expelled student would lie inside the coffin.

These were certainly pranks of both questionable taste and very big budgets. Quite how students secured funeral horses, undertakers' carts and full mourning wear wasn't always discovered.

What was frequently discovered were the culprits. Bulldogs and proctors – the University police – would often break up a mock funeral procession with some violence whenever they were encountered, and huge fines were slapped on those involved. Very few made it all the way to Oxford station. One was dismantled by the authorities having reached no further than the High.

By the beginning of the First World War, the practice had just about been curtailed in Oxford and Cambridge, though a few later occurrences of students in hearses were reported. As for the hearses, today most students wouldn't be seen dead in one!

F for Frideswide

To be accepted by both Oxford's townspeople and the University as a spiritual leader of the city, you'd need to be a saint. Fortunately Frideswide is a saint. Moreover, she is the patron saint of both Oxford city and Oxford University.

She's also quite old. We think she was born sometime in the 650s and died in the year 727. Before she became a saint, Frideswide was a princess. But she decided to abandon a royal future and instead dedicated herself to God.

She founded a priory thought to be on the site where Christ Church now stands. For her birthday present one year, she insisted that her father build her a church – which would have been really annoying if he'd already decided to buy her a pony. Frideswide may have been a tiny bit spoilt, as her father duly gifted her a new church on the outskirts of Oxford (although no one referred to the place as Oxford at that time).

In becoming an abbotess she pledged to remain unmarried and dedicate herself to Christianity. She also persuaded twelve young unmarried women to join her in founding a convent. Somewhat liberally for the age, she rejected the cloistered life and lived in clear view of the sinful world.

Which must have made it difficult for Frideswide to control her twelve young charges: 'So, like, we can stay in this draughty building all day chanting prayers, or go into the city where there's loads of hot guys and alcohol?' 'Yes, my child, that is the choice you must make by seeking God's guidance … oh, you've all gone.'

BOO BOO BOO BOO BOO BOO BOO BOO BOO BOO

However, saintly Frideswide's rejection of marriage in pursuing religious rapture did not stop the Mercian king Æthelbald (you can boo whenever you see his name) pursuing her aggressively for marriage. His dating technique was as unsuccessful as it was unrefined. He attempted to kidnap Frideswide.

Unsurprisingly, the kidnap attempt did not impress her and Frideswide made it clear that she wasn't interested in dating

Æthelbald (boo). Presumably she couldn't swipe left fast enough.

But Æthelbald (boo) wouldn't take a 'no' or, more specifically, a 'no, leave me alone, you creep' for an answer. Eventually God conveniently intervened, and legend has it that Frideswide's lecherous pursuer was struck blind with an accurately targeted divine lightning bolt. Quite how Æthelbald (boo) survived this direct lightning strike to the head is not recorded.

Somewhat charitably, given the circumstances, Frideswide agreed to perform a miracle and restore Æthelbald's (boo) sight, having first sensibly insisted that she'd only perform the miracle if he agreed to leave her alone.

BOO BOO BOO BOO BOO BOO

His pursuit of her had become so lascivious that she took to hiding in a pig sty in Binsey (a village on the Thames just north of Oxford). Which can't have been a pleasant place to live. Nor the pig sty. (Sorry, Binsey.)

While employed as a swineherd, she prayed for a fresh water well to spring up at Binsey. You can see why she'd want a wash. And God duly obliged. The well is still there today, and was adapted into 'the treacle well' by Lewis Carroll in his *Alice's Adventures in Wonderland*.

Reformed and re-sighted, Æthelbald (no longer boo) kept his side of the bargain and disappeared, leaving Frideswide to continue with her abbey life.

After her death she was entombed there, and once again numerous people failed to leave her alone: pilgrims. News of her dedication to a holy life, coupled with her spurning of an opportunity to become a real-life princess, meant that her stock rose in religious circles. Especially once her miracle had entered popular folklore.

There's little doubt that the pilgrims flocking to her tomb would have helped Oxford to grow into a sizeable town, and potentially sparked the origins of the University.

Today Frideswide's colourful story is told in a stained glass window in Christ Church cathedral. Designed by pre-Raphaelite artist Edward Burne-Jones, the panels depict Frideswide's life story – with one panel clearly displaying a plumbed-in toilet with modern flush facility. Frideswide clearly had a very advanced plumber in the eighth century! (In reality, the nineteenth-century window includes this anachronistic detail to celebrate Oxford's then newly installed sewer system.)

Frideswide is now remembered not only for her tomb in Binsey and the window in Christ Church, but also for St Frideswide's Church in Osney and Frideswide Square, the first area that visitors encounter when they emerge from Oxford railway station.

F Question?

When out walking one day, Frideswide was stopped by a horribly diseased leper. According to legend, what did Frideswide do next while her companions gasped in horror?

Ee

Oxbridge students used to have a special trophy to prove that theirs was the lowest exam mark of the academic year. The expression 'the wooden spoon' originates from the Oxbridge tradition of the achiever of the worst marks in Finals each year being presented with an elaborate spoon carved from wood.

The practice existed right up until the start of the First World War, and by then the spoons had grown so huge that they were carved from rowing oars – a sign of the recipient's dedication to the college boat rather than his academic studies.

The University did not want the railway to come to Oxford and actively campaigned against it. After all, concluded the authorities, it would bring undesirables (i.e. anyone who wasn't a member of the University) to the city.

Hence the Chancellor at the time – who was none other than the Duke of Wellington – harrumphed that the University did not want railway access to Oxford as it would 'encourage the lower orders to move around'. And Oxford had a reputation for elitism? Where does that come from?

Eventually the railway did reach Oxford in 1844. However, proctors patrolled the station to ensure that no tickets were sold to students for any destination that had a horseracing course.

E for eBay

An epic student prank was initiated in 2005 by two undergraduates at Lincoln College. The mischievous pair put hated rival Brasenose College up for sale on eBay!

Bidding was surprisingly active before eBay realised that this might not be a legitimate sale and pulled the sixteenth-century academic establishment, complete with its 500 students, from the online auction site.

The twin rapscallions were fined £50 each by the University for their prank. Alongside their fine,

the guilty Lincoln students had to endure a second punishment deemed appropriate for their crime by the unimpressed authorities. At formal hall one evening, they were paraded before Brasenose College students and made to recite the traditional Brasenose grace in Latin before dinner. That'll teach them (some Latin!) the *Lex talionis* (meaning law of retaliation). Could a punishment be more Oxford?

Oculi omnium spectant in te, Deus...

E Question?

What was the highest bid that Brasenose College attracted on eBay after pranksters from Lincoln College auctioned it as 'A used item (since 1509) with 510 students in a generally quite worn condition'?

D for Duck

All Souls is a huge college without any students – which sounds a bit odd. But not as odd as the college's duck ceremony. This tradition started when the college foundations were being dug in 1437, it's said, causing a gigantic mallard to fly out of a drain and cause, er, quite a flap.

Fellows of the esteemed college obviously thought: 'This definitely requires celebration with a huge dinner, a specially commissioned song and multitudes of booze.' So they did, and still do. There's a special mallard song that members of college sing during the occasion, when they appoint a

Lord of the Mallard (sometimes, but not always, the Warden of college) who is paraded around in a sedan chair. Fitter Fellows ascend the Codrington Library roof and sing the mallard song from behind the college's ornate Sir Christopher Wren sundial.

Participants stride around the college hunting a mallard, which makes little sense because they carry a duck on a pole which is also the one they're supposedly seeking. Nowadays they thankfully use a wooden mallard. The last time an unfortunate real mallard was impaled on a stick was in 1801. Mercifully it's been a carved duck (as in the wooden variety) ever since.

And how often does All Souls stage this bizarre ceremony of the mallard? Once every 100 years. The last one took place in 2001, meaning that the next one is scheduled for January 2101 (if you want to put it in your diary.

D for Dodo

Charles Do-do-dodgson's stutter created a famous dodo which enabled his nom de plume, Lewis Carroll, to disappear down into a world of adventure. But the dodo also really existed in Oxford too – probably the very last intact dodo ever to be seen.

Unfortunately, in 1755 an Oxford museum employee destroyed the world's only remaining dodo specimen. Subsequent retellings have no doubt embellished the story, attributing the unfortunate action to an over-zealous worker tidying up the museum.

Legend dictates that he burned the world's last remaining dodo specimen on the entrance steps. This unfortunate mistake must have come up at his annual workplace appraisal.

So the Old Ashmolean on Broad Street (now the Museum of the History of Science) definitely did hold a complete dodo specimen but destroyed it in 1755. Or at least most of it. The bird's foot and beak remain. Today they reside safely at Oxford's Natural History Museum – unless any over-keen new employee has recently had a tidy-up and a bonfire.

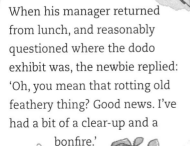

When his manager returned from lunch, and reasonably questioned where the dodo exhibit was, the newbie replied: 'Oh, you mean that rotting old feathery thing? Good news. I've had a bit of a clear-up and a bonfire.'

D for Dung

Oxford's Botanic Garden was England's first physic garden, installed two centuries before Kew Gardens in London. A physic garden is where plants with medicinal properties are grown.

In the 1620s, '4000 cartloads of muck and dunge' (dunge with an erroneous 'e', as the spelling was clearly dunge too) were required to ensure that the soil was not only fertile, but raised above the River Cherwell flowing alongside.

Henry Danvers, the Earl of Danby, presented Oxford University with five acres of land and spent £5,000 preparing the land to become a garden. Which mostly involved spreading dung(e).

He certainly wanted his garden's entrance to be ostentatious. Most people's garden gate is a tiny wooden structure with a squeaky hinge. But for his garden gate, Danvers appointed one of Britain's foremost craftsmen and Inigo Jones' master mason, a man ideally surnamed for his future profession: Nicholas Stone. Furthermore, he made the stone gate ginormous.

The high and wide stone entrance gate can still be seen today; it's hard to miss. A big statue of Danvers himself appears in the centre of the structure, flanked by Charles I on the left, and on the right Charles II mystifyingly dressed as a Roman emperor. No, I don't know why either.

But after such a big welcome, the gatehouse didn't actually offer access to anything at all. The first curator, Jacob Bobart, appointed in 1642, was simply not paid by the University. So he dug and hoed himself a living by growing fruit and vegetables that he flogged to hungry undergraduates. After a few years, the University relented on its non-funding and the physic garden began to take shape, with Bobart amassing nearly 2,000 plants. Its name changed in 1840 to today's familiar Oxford Botanic Garden.

The garden is built upon the site of the former Jewish Cemetery, which is the origin of one of Oxford's most sinister-sounding places. Dead Man's Walk takes its name from the ruling that Jews were not permitted in medieval times to be buried within Oxford city. Their funeral processions therefore had to follow the lane outside the city wall to where the Botanic Garden now stands: just beyond the formerly enclosed medieval city.

The Botanic Garden is also one of the few places in the UK licensed to grow cannabis. Thankfully its gift shop sells a selection of instant snacks - for anyone experiencing sudden hunger pangs.

D Question?

According to an information board in the Oxford Botanic Garden, what plant – grown in its garden – has probably killed more humans than any other?

C for Charles Dodgson at Christ Church

Charles Dodgson arrived in Oxford as an undergraduate in 1850. After two days, he was summoned home as his mother had died suddenly. But he soon returned to Oxford, and stayed on at Christ Church until his own death forty-eight years later.

Christ Church also owned the rectory in Cheshire where Dodgson, one of eleven children, was born. Dodgson's mathematical abilities ensured that he was offered a lectureship after graduating. Yet his lecturing skills were criticised by students for being dull and tedious.

It probably didn't help that he suffered from stammering when speaking to adults, although this reportedly disappeared in the company of children. Whenever he pronounced his surname, he involuntarily prefixed it with 'Do-do-dodgson', giving him an idea that he incorporated in his stories (see D for Dodo).

Dodgson is of course best known today for his storytelling to the daughter of the Dean of Christ Church, Alice Liddell. Though the name we know better is his nom de plume, Lewis Carroll.

One 'golden afternoon', Dodgson rowed Alice and her two sisters along the Thames from Folly Bridge to Binsey and told them a story. Alice begged him to write it down, and the result was *Alice's Adventures Under Ground*. Eventually, he settled on the superior title *Alice's Adventures in Wonderland* and it was published in 1865. Benefiting from John Tenniel's wonderful illustrations

– after Dodgson initially tried providing his own drawings – the book has never been out of print since.

The Alice stories are full of references to Christ Church – unsurprisingly, since he was there nearly all his life. The tree with the grinning cat is in the college gardens; the firedogs in the dining hall inspired the characters with hydraulic necks; and the scurrying white rabbit, always checking his watch, was based on the Dean. He was a shy man, who escaped after dinner in hall through a tiny door in the wooden panelling, so that he could return to his rooms and avoid small talk with the students.

And he always checked his pocket watch before disappearing through the hole.

Lewis Carroll, or rather Charles Dodgson, received tens of thousands of fan letters. He studiously catalogued them all, allocating each one a number in his filing system, yet he only replied to correspondents who had addressed him by his real name, not his pen name.

One huge fan of his work was Queen Victoria. She liked the Alice stories so much that she supposedly asked him for a copy of his next book. Apparently Dodgson obliged, and duly posted her an inscribed copy of his next book, *An Elementary Treatise on Determinants, with their Application to Simultaneous Linear Equations and Algebraic Equations, by Charles Dodgson*. Yet the more Dodgson persistently denied this story was true, the more people repeated it!

Later, the real Alice eventually married and became Alice Liddell Hargreaves. Initially, she shunned the attention that Dodgson's stories inevitably brought her; but in later life she fell into financial difficulties that forced her to sell the original book which Dodgson had annotated for her.

The action in *Alice's Adventures in Wonderland* occurs on 4 May – the real Alice's birthday. And, according to Dodgson, her 'non-birthday' is on any other day of the year.

C for Carfax stocks

One eighteenth-century Oxford-shire reprobate sold phony shares in a brewery, and promptly ended up in the town's stocks. As the locals pelted him with enthusiasm (as well as rotting fruit and veg), the conman could at least ponder how dodgy stocks had landed him in even worse stocks.

The permanent disappear-ance of the wooden stocks from Carfax was caused by a bizarre accident.

The townspeople were out celebrating the nation's military victory in the Crimean War of 1856. Unimpressed with the official celebrations, the locals decided to upscale the festivities and start their own bonfires. One of these fires was soon roaring out of control, destroying the town's stocks in Carfax as well as singeing the walls of St Martin's Church – of which only Carfax Tower remains standing today.

History doesn't record how the unintentional arsonists were punished – though they'd be relieved to realise that they couldn't be put in the stocks!

C for Clubs

Oxford University and its constituent colleges have many dining clubs. Several have ancient origins; some are notorious for debauchery. Others, like Vincent's, have been the location for world records.

This sporty club played host to Bob Hawke – then a Rhodes Scholar at University College, but later Prime Minister of Australia – at the Turf Tavern in 1963. He achieved the world record in sconcing. (If advised to take up a sport by your doctor, it's probably best not to opt for sconcing.)

Sconcing means consuming a yard of ale (approx. 1.5 litres) from a trumpet-shaped drinking vessel in the shortest time possible. Hawke achieved this 'distinction' in a world record of eleven seconds. Good to see future politicians encouraging responsible consumption. Ironically his parents were strict members of the temperance movement. Hawke's mother often carried a damaged liver in a jar to lecture against alcohol.

Just to show that Oxford's various clubs cannot be accused of clinging to old-fashioned values out of step with modernity, this same Vincent's finally voted to accept women as members in, er, 2016!

Oxford's Zenith Dining Club was founded in 1902. At their inaugural dinner, the students decided to smash up the restaurant.

This led to all ten members being permanently sent down from Oxford and the club discontinued. Which leaves an impressive Zenith Club record: Number of members: ten. Number of permanent exclusions from Oxford: ten. Number of dinners in the dining club's history: one.

Members of the notorious Bullingdon Club once smashed over 400 windows in Peckwater Quad in Christ Church in 1894; and then smashed 400 more in 1927. On hearing of their subsequent expulsion from college, one club member arrogantly replied:

'My father is in the Cabinet, so we'll all be back by Monday – you'll see!'

They weren't back on Monday – or any other day. Ha!

C for Crocodile

An Oxford club founded by John Buchan (who would later write the famous novel *The Thirty-Nine Steps*) had an oddly specific name: the Crocodile Club.

The future author, then an undergraduate at Brasenose College, sensibly wrote down the club's rules in 1896. The Crocodile Club had two main rules. 1: No one is eligible for membership who has a serious stain on his moral character. (Very sensible.) 2: All meetings shall take place in a room with a real crocodile present throughout. (Not very sensible.)

This might have rendered the club's first meeting a Health and Safety nightmare. Although sourcing a crocodile in the first place ought to have proved tricky.

Demonstrating a typical student approach to packing only the essentials for a term in Oxford, a Brasenose undergrad went to his room and immediately returned with a real crocodile (albeit of the stuffed variety). Hence the Crocodile Club could begin.

During a meeting of the Crocodile Club in 1921, a member observed that the crocodile present was in fact an alligator. True to its principles, the club immediately disbanded, vowing not to reconvene until an actual crocodile was present. The club has not met since.

C Question?

Let's ask a C for Cambridge question (mainly because the answer makes Cambridge look bad!). Oxford University finally allowed women to obtain degrees in 1920. What year did Cambridge University first award degrees to women? (a) 1908 (b) 1928 (c) 1948

B for Brasenose

Brasenose is a college named after a doorknocker. And that's only half the story!

Although officially founded in 1509, Brasenose College has much earlier origins. It occupies the site of the thirteenth-century scholastic institution, Brasenose Hall. Alas, these were not peaceful times. In fact, Oxford was downright dangerous during this period of history.

In 1333 yet another Town v. Gown riot had exploded on the streets. Brasenose Hall students, including the wonderfully named Philippus le Maniciple (I'm guessing with a name like that his route to Oxford wasn't as part of a state school outreach programme), had been caught administering some serious blows – some say fatal – to equally belligerent townspeople.

Fearing reprisals from an angry town mob gathering outside Brasenose's wooden gates, with the evident plan of splintering them, the students decided to leave Oxford hastily and flee the mob.

Before absconding, they only had time to pack the essentials: clothes, money and... a large brass ornamental door knocker. But they did manage to make their getaway just in time before the revenge-fixated Town mob stormed Brasenose looking for the culprits.

Once the escapees had got as far north as Lincolnshire, they decided they'd fled far enough to be safe. They stayed in Stamford, started their own Oxford-like educational establishment and hung the stolen doorknocker on their new gate.

But there was a problem. A problem of royal proportions. The king was not in favour of this student migration to Stamford, and Edward II ordered them back to Oxford. Since it was a royal decree, they agreed to return to Oxford.

But they must have had even less time for packing before they departed, as this time they forgot the door knocker and left it in Stamford.

Here it remained for over 500 years until 1890, when Brasenose House, now a school in Stamford, was put up for sale.

Brasenose College asked for its doorknocker back. The school refused, saying that if Brasenose wanted its precious doorknocker so much, then it would have to buy the entire school. 'Ha!' thought the school, no doubt; 'that'll teach those stuck-up Oxford college types.' So Brasenose did purchase the whole school, just to reclaim its eponymous doorknocker.

The original doorknocker now sits quietly in the main hall at Brasenose, and a replica can be found adorning the college gate in Radcliffe Square.

Right up until the nineteenth century, Oxford University still deemed it necessary for all Oxford students receiving an MA to swear an oath pledging 'not to lecture in Stamford'.

B for Béjaune

Béjaune is a French word imported, like the custom it describes, into Oxford. The word signified a rather malicious initiation ceremony that new Oxford students were forced to endure a long time ago.

Freshers in fifteenth-century Oxford as well as French and German universities could look forward to initiation rituals involving vast quantities of alcohol to be consumed (that the unfortunate fresher would be made to pay for), before being pelted with rotten shellfish. Sometimes throwers didn't provide the fresher with the kindness of removing the smelly crustaceans from their hard shells first.

Things could and did get worse. The initiate was then banged repeatedly over the head with a frying pan. It would vary at which stage the student decided that studying at Oxford was definitely overrated.

B for Bread: 'Give us our daily riot'

Oxford's history, as we've seen, been beset by regular Town v. Gown riots. Yet the city's last truly epic-scale riot took place a safe time ago: 1867. It erupted because of a University price rise enforced on the town's shops.

The rumpus resulted from local people's frustration over bread prices. Incredible as it is to imagine today, the price of a

bread loaf in Oxford was once decided by the University. And when a hefty price hike was announced, leaving many of Oxford's poor feeling fearful as to how they'd continue to earn a crust, their annoyance ignited into an explosive riot.

These disturbances were so violent that a regiment of soldiers was brought from Windsor to Oxford. Billeted in the city, they were then issued with live ammunition to patrol the streets. Some rich Oxford students gave speeches calling for bread prices to remain high! Needless to say, this didn't help to calm the situation but provoked the rioters even more. From the balcony of Oxford's Town Hall the townspeople were read the Riot Act. Quite literally.

Eventually the rioting was quelled. But only after the University agreed to back down and lower the price of bread. And how much was the price increase that led to such violent riots? One penny!

B for Beggars

Not every student at Oxford was rich. Between 1551 and 1571, Oxford University issued a special licence to twenty-three students permitting them to beg.

B for Bridge of Sighs

Arguably the most photographed landmark in Oxford, the Bridge of Sighs is surprisingly not what it seems. Firstly, it isn't even called the Bridge of Sighs (yes, I'm aware I've just called it that twice already). Its actual name is Hertford Bridge, which is perfectly logical since it bridges two separate parts of the same college: Hertford.

Furthermore, in spite of every tourist taking a photo of this iconic construction, it's actually not that old. In fact it's shamelessly twentieth-century, built in 1913. In 2013 students held a 100th birthday party under the bridge, and even baked a cake with 100 candles.

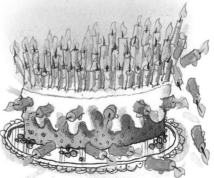

Initially the college was founded in the thirteenth century as Hart College. Years later it started crumbling into the street (that really happened), and was reformed as Hertford College in 1740. Now it can count successful alumni including Jonathan Swift, Evelyn Waugh, Fiona Bruce and Soweto Kinch.

Those tourists snapping photos might also be surprised about the purpose of the bridge. In the first few years of the twentieth century, the annex buildings of Hertford were erected across the street. Largely to provide new toilets. The

covered walkway was installed to protect sensitive students from getting wet on their visits to the facilities.

The Bridge of Sighs (or, yes, you're quite right: Hertford Bridge) is staggeringly unoriginal. The original Bridge of Sighs is in Venice and is said to have adopted its name from prisoners sighing as they crossed the bridge from prison cells to their place of execution. There is also a Bridge of Sighs in Cambridge and a replica version in a casino in Las Vegas.

The best true story is maybe the one about a tourist who recently asked the way to the river in Oxford; when asked which part of the river, he said he was looking for the Bridge of Sighs!

Oxford and Cambridge have been contesting the Boat Race since 1829. Throughout this time, there has been only one dead-heat. It happened in 1877 – and the controversy has yet to recede. The finishing line judge, known appropriately as 'Honest' John Phelps, declared that the two crews were inseparable at the finish. This was not a view shared by anyone else present, including the correspondent from *Punch* magazine who quoted Phelps as saying: 'A dead heat to Oxford by five feet!

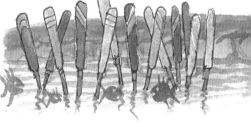

Still, it could have been worse. In the 1912 race, both crews sank!

B Question?

WHERE'S THE RIVER?

Although the Boat Race has been rowed over a similar stretch of the Thames in London since 1845, the very first race in 1829 took place in neither London, Oxford nor Cambridge, but where?

A for Answers

Firstly, let's have an A QUESTION. After all, we can't have A ANSWER without A QUESTION. So here are three abbreviations much used by Oxford students.

What are these student words short for: Tute? Clunch? Plodge? (*Answer at the end, after Z.*)

B ANSWER: Henley-on-Thames, about 25 miles south-east of Oxford.

C ANSWER: Shamefully it was not until after the Second World War in 1948, and even then it was only an honorary degree awarded to the Queen Mother (presumably for wearing jolly hats in public).

D ANSWER: Tobacco. So don't smoke, kids!

Tute...

...Clunch...

Plodge?

Oxford has an interesting botanic claim to fame. It is responsible for covering most of Britain with a yellow daisy-like flower. It's even named after the city. Although the plant is native to the volcanic soil of Sicily's Mount Etna, seventeeth-century plant hunters snaffled seeds and planted them in the Botanic Garden.

Airborne seeds soon escaped and the flower was spotted growing on college walls – where it was duly christened 'Oxford ragwort'.

But it took the coming of the railway to spread the flower from Oxford to the rest of the nation. Since clinker beds on the railway tracks replicate the plant's favourite environment of volcanic lava fields, the yellow flowers were soon spotted everywhere along the railway line from Oxford, first reaching Didcot, and then quickly beyond.

E ANSWER: Bidding reached £10 million – plus £20 postage and packaging!

F ANSWER: She kissed the leper and his skin immediately became smooth and disease-free.

G ANSWER: A wooden chimney. I'll say that again, he had a WOODEN chimney! He probably owned a chocolate fireguard too.

H ANSWER: Pirate. They really did both leave Oxford after graduation to become pirates. It's fair to say that the Oxford University Careers Department needed to up their game in that era!

I ANSWER: King Richard I was born in Oxford in 1157 and King John in 1167.

Other famous people born in Oxford include Hugh Laurie, Stephen Hawking, David Oyelowo, Dorothy L Sayers, Louis Hynes, KT Franklin, Florence Pugh, Miriam Margolyes and, possibly, Nell Gwyn – famous actress and mistress of King Charles II.

J ANSWER: They all left Oxford without getting a degree. So who says you need a degree to get on in life?

K ANSWER: King Charles I really was the shortest royal monarch. Even before they cut his head off! (What, too soon? 1649?)

L ANSWER: His removed appendix.

M ANSWER: A likely cause was putting a stop to a massive brain drain of Oxford academics emigrating to Australia Both Sydney and Melbourne universities were established in the mid-nineteenth century with dons expelled from Oxford after their secret marriages and families were discovered.

N ANSWER: Kermit the Frog. He spoke for nearly ten minutes – longer than some famous humans managed when asked to address the Oxford Union.

O ANSWER: Captain Scott took tins of Oxford Marmalade on his ill-fated expedition to the Antarctic in 1910. Scott died in 1912, but in

1980 a perfectly preserved tin of Frank Cooper's famous delicacy was found in Scott's last hut where he froze to death.

P ANSWER: The answer is that the Nobel committee only awards a maximum of three prizes for each discovery, so if you're working on a major world-changing science discovery, make sure you don't have more than three people in your team. Or prepare to fall out with your colleagues!

Q ANSWER: The Queen's College, located in Oxford's High Street. While studying for his degree, Rowan Atkinson joined the Oxford University Drama Society, and began to develop his Mr Bean character. The idea came to him of a 'strange, surreal and non-speaking character' as he stood in front of his mirror pulling faces.

R ANSWER: He was rusticated (that's a posh Oxford word for suspended) for a mere fortnight.

S ANSWER: He set its tail on fire. (Later a horse was responsible for Foote losing a leg – in a probable case of animal karma!)

T ANSWER: October. With the clocks spinning backwards every year to alter BST to GMT, October is 31 days and one hour long. But if you said September, then that's good too – given that it's nine letters long!

U ANSWER: Only four. There haven't been many Chancellors in Oxford's history as they often occupy the role for a long time. Like most Popes, the role tends to be for life.